EDUCATING
THE TUDORS

To Pops, thank you for everything, this is for you.

EDUCATING THE TUDORS

AMY McELROY

PEN & SWORD
HISTORY

AN IMPRINT OF PEN & SWORD BOOKS LTD.
YORKSHIRE - PHILADELPHIA

First published in Great Britain in 2023 by
PEN AND SWORD HISTORY
An imprint of
Pen & Sword Books Ltd
Yorkshire – Philadelphia

ISBN 978 1 39909 596 9

A CIP catalogue record for this book is available from the British Library.

Typeset in Times New Roman 12/16 by
SJmagic DESIGN SERVICES, India.
Printed and bound in the UK by CPI Group (UK) Ltd.

Pen & Sword Books Limited incorporates the imprints of Atlas, Archaeology,
Aviation, Discovery, Family History, Fiction, History, Maritime, Military, Military
Classics, Politics, Select, Transport, True Crime, Air World, Frontline Publishing,
Leo Cooper, Remember When, Seaforth Publishing, The Praetorian Press,
Wharncliffe Local History, Wharncliffe Transport, Wharncliffe True Crime and
White Owl.

For a complete list of Pen & Sword titles please contact
PEN & SWORD BOOKS LIMITED
47 Church Street, Barnsley, South Yorkshire, S70 2AS, England
E-mail: enquiries@pen-and-sword.co.uk
Website: www.pen-and-sword.co.uk

Or

PEN AND SWORD BOOKS
1950 Lawrence Rd, Havertown, PA 19083, USA
E-mail: Uspen-and-sword@casematepublishers.com
Website: www.penandswordbooks.com

Contents

Acknowledgements

I never for a second thought I would ever be writing my own acknowledgements but here I am. There are many who I would like to thank, the first being my Dad. Thanks, Pops, for all the support you have given me through the years, I couldn't have done this without your encouragement, I love you. Thanks also to Lindsay who shares my love of history.

Colin and Sarah, thank you for the continued support, and yes Colin I know this will probably be the only page you read but that's ok!

This has been a crazy journey, writing my first book amidst a pandemic was never going to be easy but there are a few that have kept me going especially Bec, thank you for all the chats, idea swapping and for being that calming influence whenever I started panicking, you are an absolute star! I could not miss out Sarah-Beth, as this journey would not have even started without you so a huge thank you for giving me the confidence to take the first step.

Thank you to my dearest friends, Lucy-Bug and Kate, you both kept me motivated, you knew better than I did that I could do this so thank you for believing in me. Michelle, thank you for being a sounding board and for the adventures. I am sure a couple of the images will bring back memories and I look forward to more adventures in the future. I also need to thank Andy (I told you I would) for listening to my IT panics and preventing me from throwing my laptop out the window!

Friends, and those who have supported me on Twitter, thank you from the bottom of my heart, it's been incredible to receive such encouragement from authors I admire so much, especially MJ, Tony and the Pen & Sword family.

I'm sure all my colleagues are probably hoping this will be the end of me wittering on now about the Tudors so I may as well apologise now, that will not happen but thank you for all the support you have given me along the way.

Special thanks to Ludlow Castle and St Lawrence Church, Ludlow and to all the museums who have kindly let me use images.

Introduction

Education during the Tudor era was not a transparent affair, it took the form of social learning as well as academic study. Children had opportunities to gain an education, from schools, within households and through apprenticeships. This might seem similar to today's educational opportunities but not all were fortunate enough to receive a formal education as attending school was not compulsory. Many children instead learnt through working or imitation of their elders. Education was also largely dependent on class. Whereas some schools today remain elite this was much more prevalent in the Tudor era. Class was not the only barrier to education; gender also determined the type and extent of education received.

In the Medieval period, education was the focus of men of the Church and was largely practical. These men held the monopoly on learning and were employed in roles where an education was required including positions within the royal court. Many cathedrals and monasteries had schools attached and grammar schools founded by guilds or individuals were already in situ before the Tudors ascended the throne. Most of the schools initially attached to cathedrals came under the responsibility of the chancellor as schools of theology and canon law. Under the Tudors, education was impacted by the Renaissance and the Reformation as well as shifting social structures and men of learning had wider opportunities than were available in Medieval times.

For most children, their early education was the responsibility of their mothers to provide. Up until the age of approximately six or seven, all children were looked after by women, including the beginning of their education and even the clothing of boys and girls was the same. At the age of six or seven, however, education changed for all children as this age was thought to mark the end of infancy. The education of girls was more functional than academic, the main aim being to learn to run their household and have a successful marriage. Boys' education focused on improving them whilst both would learn the basics of religion and decorum.

All Tudor children regardless of social class had to learn a complex set of social behaviours and rules. These rules helped them interact with others whatever their status and taught them to obey their elders. Sumptuary Laws dictated colours and fabrics an individual could wear according to rank, for instance only royals could wear purple. Children would be expected to learn to distinguish a person's rank from their clothing. Posture was also an indication of a person's social standing and children would be taught how to identify a person's rank not only through their clothing but their posture and thereby how to address and behave towards them. Boys were expected to grow up to be bold and assertive whilst girls were meant to be gentle and conform to their father's and later, their husband's, wishes. Children would be taught from an early age how to show deference including bowing for boys and curtseying for girls. At a very young age, boys would be expected to doff their cap with a small bow while girls would perform a small dipping motion until they could perform a curtsey. Certain behaviours were forbidden such as wiping your nose on your sleeve which is difficult to envision young children remembering especially those of the lower classes who might not have handkerchiefs of their own. Eating with your mouth full and resting elbows were also forbidden and all children would be expected to remember this etiquette. It would be particularly enforced in the homes of the aristocracy where children were brought up as miniature adults.

Just like today, schools and universities were not the only institutions to provide education, children could be educated through apprenticeships and on-the-job learning. There were various types of schools but most, at the beginning of the period were run by the Church as literacy and learning were considered necessary for those pursuing an ecclesiastical career. In small villages or towns with no school, a priest was often paid to teach the local children or a wealthy member of the community might retain a tutor for all children providing the tutor with accommodation and space to teach. Even if, 'free' schools were present, it did not mean the whole experience was free. Parents would still be responsible for ensuring their child had materials to write with and might have been expected to contribute towards the costs of running the school. For the purposes of this work, 'free' will refer to the cost of admission and not any other costs incurred.

The term 'school' during the Tudor period referred to all educational establishments, even universities were known as schools and to indicate the difference they would be referred to either by the grade of study, curriculum or constitution. Examples of grade could be elementary, grammar or higher. Constitution would refer to who controlled and supported the school, for example, a monastic or chantry school and lastly, curriculum could mean grammar or theology amongst others. The schools were referred to differently by individuals and the references interchangeable for example a specific grammar school supported by a monastery could be referred to by its grade (grammar), constitution (monastery supported grammar school) or curriculum (grammar).[1] There were essentially four tiers of education; elementary, secondary, degree and lastly, the higher arts. What we would call elementary schools had various names including almonry, petty, monastic and song amongst others. Grammar schools largely formed today's version of secondary school and the university colleges or Inns of Court provided the third and fourth tiers of education.

Petty schools were also known as ABC schools and aimed to teach local children their alphabet, spelling and reading. Some petty schools benefitted from the ability to teach writing and basic counting skills as well but this was not common. Almonry and song schools were initially established to provide an education to poor boys training for the choir but they also accepted sons of the gentry. Acting as a tutor provided priests with an additional income to supplement the small payments received for the saying of masses for the souls of wealthy benefactors. The boys in almonry schools were taught to sing and might have also received an elementary education or at least basic reading and writing skills. Monasteries tended to have their own training schools for novices wishing to become monks. These training schools were sometimes connected to an almonry school. Education was not the sole priority for monasteries, they had other obligations of providing hospitality for pilgrims or the wealthy, offering medical care, growing produce and of course, carrying out prayer and religious observances.

Chantry schools were attached to churches before their dissolution in 1547, chantry priests could be paid a fee to educate the local children when they were not singing masses for the founder of the chantry chapel as they did not have any other parochial responsibilities. Foundations of secular canons were generally more concerned with education than those founded by monasteries which aimed to produce those entering the Church or religious orders. Secular foundations usually included grammar schools and theological schools. Grammar schools mostly fell under the control of a master whereas theological schools fell under the jurisdiction of the chancellor.

At the beginning of the period, grammar schools were mostly founded by guilds, sometimes in connection with colleges, with a view that the pupils would advance to that college, but as education prospered the founding of grammar schools by wealthy individuals became more common. The aim of the grammar school was to instil knowledge of the theory and practice of grammar to enable boys to understand, speak and write eloquently. Throughout the period the study of grammar included the languages of English, Latin and Greek with the majority of grammar schools focusing on Latin literature. Collegiate churches originally were independent buildings but began to have chapels added to them. Boys could board at these schools whilst those not fortunate enough to afford to board or attend might have been able to receive some learning in exchange for completing chores. King's College, Cambridge was one such college that was founded in connection to a grammar school. It was founded in connection to Eton, providing an establishment for boys to continue their studies.

As with the differences in schools, the knowledge and skill of those teaching also varied. Some priests and clerks who were teaching had just enough Latin to be able to teach young children the basics whilst headmasters of a grammar school might be highly educated with a degree from Oxford, Cambridge or one of the renowned universities abroad such as Padua, Italy. Tutors and schoolmasters also held differing opinions on the use of corporal punishment. Whilst it was certainly present in schools not all tutors were supportive of its use and argued against it, instead, preferring to treat pupils with kindness. It might be surprising to note that class did not save a child from such punishment, although some did employ another child to suffer the punishment on their behalf known as a 'whipping boy'.

During the fifteenth century, the number of schools increased in England but the curriculum largely remained unaltered. Grammar schools and universities concentrated on the seven liberal arts, grammar school provided the *trivium* – grammar, rhetoric and dialectic and the universities provided the *quadrivium* – arithmetic, geometry, astronomy and music. Towards the latter part of the century when the Tudor's came to the throne 'New Learning' was increasing in significance in Europe. Whilst it is termed 'new' it was far from it, it was actually the study of rediscovered writings and languages which had begun in Italy. Various ancient manuscripts by Greek and Latin philosophers such as Aristotle, Plato, Marcus Tullius Cicero and Quintilian who were writing during the time of the Roman Republic and Empire were discovered, and became the focus of great interest amongst scholars. A number of scholars, particularly in Italy took on the task of translating the works known as classics and some took the opportunity to search for more, travelling across

Europe in the hopes of finding a forgotten work by one of these great writers. In the fifteenth century, a school was formed in Italy to focus on Greek literature and soon after the interest in classical Latin and Greek spread across Europe. The study of classical Latin and Greek developed as part of the Renaissance, giving scholars the opportunity to study ancient texts and the scriptures through learning ancient languages as opposed to the colloquial Latin that was common at the time. The Renaissance was a large cultural and social movement across Europe and included art, music, architecture and learning, of which Humanism formed the literary aspect. A humanist was an individual who studied *studia humanitatis* which consisted of studying the classical authors to learn a curriculum including but limited to, grammar, rhetoric, philosophy and history. It brought a revival of learning with different subjects and a new breed of scholars to the forefront of education in England and across Europe, becoming known as the 'New Learning'. The liberal arts remained the curriculum for many but the teaching methods might have altered, or the material studied differed from previously as the discovered works led to an immense amount of literature previously unknown in Europe. For some, this meant reviewing the current ideals regarding education and evaluating these against the ancient works. As interest in the 'New Learning' increased ideas developed around the nature of Christianity and humanists began to prioritise the study of classical Latin and Greek, with the philosophical works of Aristotle and Plato amongst others, leading the way. It was not just scholars that sought out ancient texts and began to learn the ancient languages including a purer form of Latin, Greek and some Hebrew. Men of the Church also sought this knowledge, as did the aristocracy. The aims of these circles were undoubtedly different; scholars wished to learn as much as they could to improve their own knowledge but also keep up with the fashionable trend sweeping Europe and have the ability to pass on their learning, ecclesiasts wished to understand religious texts from their source which would enable them to improve their religious works and preaching, and the aristocracy wished to appear learned in their social groups with the hope of advancement.

Humanists did not wish to merely change the curriculum but also believed that through the correct learning, a child could be modelled with the correct morals and behaviours. Many agreed with the theories of the classical writer, Quintilian in his work *Institutio Oratoria* that a child should be introduced to education gradually from elementary learning to a school by the age of seven. The study of this and other works led to scholarly debates and further writings, in particular the differences between Aristotle and Plato's theories. Aristotle had originally been a pupil of Plato but began to develop his own theories and wrote an immense number of works covering subjects from philosophy, logic, ethics, politics and rhetoric. Plato was taught by Socrates and became the founder of the first educational establishment in the west, therefore, due to their immense influence on the 'New Learning', there was likely not a single scholar who studied philosophy without reading some of their work and both are still read to this day. Many humanists sought to study these works for their own knowledge but the leading humanists of the day also sought to reform education through introducing new methods of learning and the understanding of humans to help them reach their potential.

History and oratory became hugely popular, in particular the history of the Roman Empire and the authors writing at that time. *History of the Peloponnesian War* by Thucydides was first printed in Latin in Italy in 1483 and became a popular work of the study of war and politics whilst Cicero was the fundamental author on oratory and Livy's *History of Rome* the favourite amongst history scholars. By reading history, children could find role models to imitate and learn from their actions whether this was a scholar, saint or military hero. It became fashionable to be educated but also created new opportunities, especially under the Tudors. The number of grammar schools began to increase, encompassing the humanist curriculum, as wealthy benefactors comprising the guilds, merchants and nobility who were all desirous to endow schools to provide education to their local communities. The universities were slower to incorporate the new curriculum but did so in the sixteenth century. The traditional curriculum of universities focused on canon and civil law, and the use of Latin to study theology whereas humanism instead focused on studying the ancient writings of history, poetry and philosophy in purified Greek and Latin. Latin was known as the 'vulgar' as it was taught as a language to be spoken, collections of colloquies were known as 'vulgars' or 'vulgaria' and were used to teach children to speak Latin. The literary Latin used by the ancient writers was a different type of Latin that many humanist scholars and tutors began to adopt in their own writing and teaching. That is not to say these colloquial collections ceased to be used, they remained in use throughout the period but emphasis shifted towards understanding the Latin of the ancient authors. The Inns of Court were another avenue of education and became popular institutes for the study of common law but not all who attended sought a career in law and instead treated the Inns as a finishing school for their education.

As education blossomed, many grammar schools were founded or endowed by wealthy patrons, nobility and royalty in the sixteenth century. Clergy and scholars, who travelled abroad to learn new languages, founded schools upon their return to England, introducing a linguistic foundation to the curriculum of the grammar schools. St Paul's School in London was founded in 1509-1510 by John Colet, Dean of St Paul's and became the model for all other grammar schools. The school was to provide free education for 153 boys but by 1525 had exceeded this number.[2] Until the sixteenth century, most schools taught in the 'vulgar', but as education flourished, they began to teach in the vernacular of English. Latin remained the international language of the Church as well as that used by scholars and diplomats so it remained an integral part of education if a person wished to pursue a career. Latin was also more highly regarded if a person could not only speak the language but also read and write in Latin.

It indicated a better education and this inference would remain under the Tudors even as more and more children were schooled. Therefore, we need to bear in mind that when discussing the study of the ancient (classical) writings, the students would be studying them in Latin and not English. English versions might have become available later but certainly scholars including men of the Church, royalty and the aristocracy would have read them in Latin and possibly Greek if they studied the language. Colet introduced a new educational system and attempted to improve schooling. Originally schoolrooms were crowded with all ages mixed. Colet split his classes into ages, appointing a master for each and removed learning of grammatical rules instead thinking that children would learn this through the study and imitation of classical authors.

Universities and colleges, traditionally, were only attended by those wishing to pursue a career with the Church or within law. With the increase in humanism, these establishments began to attract the gentry and other lay persons who wished to pursue specific careers or a position at the royal court in which subjects such as history would assist them. The colleges at Oxford and Cambridge were largely staffed by regent masters, that is, those who had graduated there and non-regent masters who were members of colleges or religious houses. By the end of the sixteenth century, the majority of people would have been receiving a humanist education with the exception of some lower classes who had no access to a humanist tutor.[3] The leading humanist scholar of the day was Desiderius Erasmus who is still renowned to this day for his works and although he was never retained as a tutor to any of the royal children, he did tutor William Blount, 4th Baron Mountjoy and also taught at university. Erasmus had a huge influence on education in England and particularly on Henry VIII himself. Humanism in England was fairly new at the beginning of the Tudor reign so the tutors initially recruited by Henry VII were indeed esteemed as they would introduce humanism to the royal family and in turn, contribute to its spread across England and its educational establishments.

As well as this, Henry VII sought to introduce an innovative educational establishment to the royal household by employing distinctive schoolmasters of reputation through either academic achievements or poets. A poet might seem an odd choice as a tutor but the two poets selected were actually poet-laureates which effectively meant they had a degree in rhetoric and versification denoting they were accomplished scholars and not just poets. Those employed in the royal household were all distinguished individuals with humanist inclinations. Royalty prior to this often focused, but not limited, a boy's education on martial expertise such as hunting, jousting along with skills in courtly entertainments including music and dancing. The Tudors continued to ensure children learnt these things but also focused on a more academic education to complement the physical aspects of education. Henry VIII is known for promoting men from humble backgrounds to significant roles within his household and council. This was a further incentive for members of the upper classes and gentry to pursue their education to the fullest in the hopes of reaching the royal household and the Privy Council.

Another key aspect of education in the Tudor times was the printing press. Before the introduction of the printing presses, those wishing to read would have to borrow or commission a manuscript. These manuscripts were beautiful works, often illuminated with images but could take a great deal of time for a scribe to complete as all were handwritten. They could also be very costly as parchment was the preferred material for manuscripts even once paper became available and provided a cheaper alternative to parchment. To commission a manuscript at the time meant either locating a copy to be copied or enlisting someone to do so on your behalf. Many still chose to purchase or commission manuscripts even after the introduction of the printing press as they were more exclusive, beautiful and displayed a sign of wealth. Henry VII's mother, Lady Margaret Beaufort, was a renowned patron of the printing press and of education. She founded Christ's College and St John's College in

Cambridge. The Tudor monarchs followed in her footsteps placing great renown on education and scholars, patronising learning and founding schools. Although printed books were available in England in the 1460s, just before the accession of the Tudors, William Caxton is remembered as the most prominent owner of the printing press, establishing himself in London in 1476. Caxton initially printed translations of poetry, didactic and religious works whilst Oxford University Press, founded in 1478, began to print theological works and bible interpretations. Caxton's target audience was the wealthy classes whilst the University's books were aimed at academics and were printed in Latin. Printing presses not only made scholarly works more readily available and more affordable but did so for all books, impacting the dissemination of literacy as a whole. As books became more readily available and education increased, the demand for books in English and other languages also increased. Previously, books had been written in Latin, the language of scholars and the clergy, across the continent. This meant regardless of where they were, they could speak to other scholars or clergy without translation. However, for those who did not have the resources to become fluent in Latin this impacted their reading until English books were produced. Books teaching the rules of composition, phrases and words were produced which were called grammars. These were mainly written by scholars and could be obtained in various languages but became very popular in English as the number of grammar schools increased. Largely, even with the printing presses, education was mostly taught in oral lessons especially in elementary and grammar school as the cost of books for classwork remained expensive except for the very wealthy.

At the beginning of the Tudor era, it is estimated only 1% of women and 5% of men could write which by the end of the sixteenth century had increased to 10% and 25% respectively, which indicates just how much education and learning grew through this period.[4] By the end of the Tudor reign, education was firmly implemented within society and no longer confined to only the wealthy or those seeking ecclesiastical careers. The Tudor monarchs were well educated as will be seen in the following chapters, but they also wished their subjects to have the same opportunities and so were determined to leave behind a legacy in education. Many schools were founded or refounded under the Tudors, some of which remain visible today such as all the King Edward VI schools as well as various colleges within the universities.

Under the Tudors, it is clear that education prospered. The Renaissance brought new scholars and fresh ideas adding a new directive to those studying the scriptures following the rediscovery of Greek. Humanists began to study not just the scriptures but all aspects of behaviour which although for some resulted in clashes with the Church, also led to the expansion of education and a wider curriculum. The printing presses brought reading to a wider audience as they reduced the cost of books but also expanded the number of books published in English. This is of particular importance as the lower classes were very unlikely to be literate in Latin, the international language used by ambassadors, courtiers, scholars and the clergy. Education prior to the Renaissance was essentially about preparing children for adulthood, ensuring they had models to base conversations on and could function in different social settings. The aristocracy would go a step further and be required to know their history, legends, and saints so they could follow their examples. The Renaissance enabled individuals to study a wider range of interests that were not just for the purpose of a career.

The following chapters will look at how people were taught, who by and what they learnt, but will also look at how religion, literature and pastimes influenced learning.

Chapter One

Educating Henry

The future Henry VIII was born 28 June 1491 at Greenwich Palace, the third child and second son of Henry VII and Elizabeth of York. As the spare heir, Henry was never intended to reign but would have been expected to support his brother as king. As a royal prince, Henry was certain to receive an excellent education, as accorded by his rank and was to become a Renaissance Prince, well educated, an accomplished musician and a fine sportsman. As the elder son, Arthur was heir to the throne and his education was documented in much more detail than that of his younger brother Henry. It is likely Henry's education would have been a similar if slightly less comprehensive version of Arthur's education. His curriculum is largely inferred from those appointed to tutor him and from letters and records written by those surrounding him.

After his christening, Henry was sent to Eltham Palace to join his elder sister, Margaret under the care of Elizabeth Denton, head of the royal nursery. Their elder brother Arthur resided elsewhere with his own staff and had already begun his education and was expected to learn to rule within his own household. Elizabeth of York and Henry's grandmother Lady Margaret Beaufort took a keen interest in the education of all the children and it is thought to have been Elizabeth of York who taught Henry to read and write.[1] With influence from her mother-in-law, Elizabeth of York was involved in the selecting of tutors and companions for her children. Henry's grandmother was very pious and is said to have worn the uncomfortable undergarment of a hair shirt. She also took vows of chastity even when married. With the influence of his father and grandmother, Henry possibly learnt his piety from an early age and would later hear Mass several

1

times per day. As a youth he had given his servant William Thomas a prayer roll which was a piece of parchment containing devotions and illuminations, to be used in prayer.

From records it is easy to assume that Henry learnt to ride at a very early age as his father paid for horses for Henry before he was three years old and he arrived at his installation as Duke of York on 1 November 1494, aged three, atop a warhorse, an impressive accomplishment for one so young.[2] Henry would be taught manners and courtesy from a young age like every other child but as a royal prince he and his siblings would all need to learn how to greet their father according to their gender; dropping to one knee for Arthur and Henry and a deep curtsey for Margaret and Mary. They would learn how to greet others corresponding to rank and how to present or accept gifts which for the princes meant removing and holding their hat in one hand and presenting the gift with the other and for the princesses would mean presenting the gift from their position in a curtsey. It was a complex set of rules for all children to learn behaviour, addresses and greetings for different ranks but even more complex for royal children who would have to learn from a very young age.

Henry's first tutor was the orator-poet, John Skelton, who was appointed between 1496 and 1498 and would move into Henry's household when his young charge was between five and seven years old. It was also in 1496 that for the first time there are records of Henry receiving a book, most likely a primer to help Henry learn his ABC and prayers and was likely illuminated or illustrated with woodcut pictures.[3] A primer was the equivalent of an elementary textbook. It would often contain the alphabet followed by basic prayers and liturgical devotions. Once a child had mastered the alphabet, they could advance to learning prayers such as the Paternoster (Lord's Prayer) and Ave Maria. Skelton regarded this appointment as a high honour and would later write a poem about his appointment;

The honour of England I learned to spell,
In dignity role that doth excel
Note and mark well this parcel
I gave him drink of the sugared well
Of Helicon's waters crystalline
Acquainting him with the Muses nine.
It comes…well [for] me to remorde [recall]
That creausner [tutor] was [I] to thy sovereign lord.
It pleases that [a] noble prince royal
Me as his master for to call
In his learning primordial'[4]

Though Skelton claims the credit of teaching Henry to spell, it is probable Henry had already begun to read and write under the supervision of Elizabeth of York but no doubt Henry's writing improved under Skelton. By seven years old Henry would already be writing on parchment using a quill and had already likely started learning the basics of Latin and French. Skelton would build on the foundations laid by Elizabeth of York to ensure Henry's knowledge and understanding of the vernacular was solid before building on his knowledge of Latin. Henry would have begun learning Latin at a young age as it was still the universal language of scholars, diplomacy and religion and as royalty, he would be required to be proficient in reading religious texts, understand Mass and other religious services as well as being able to read manuscripts and documents sent by foreign princes and ambassadors. Henry VII had not learned Latin and had to rely on his Latin secretary to translate for him so he likely would have wanted to ensure his children were fluent and did not have to rely on others as he had. Under the guidance of Skelton, it is probable Henry would have undertaken a classic curriculum based on the seven liberal arts, delivered in a humanist method as Skelton believed learning should be enjoyable. Henry would have first undertaken the *trivium* – Latin grammar, rhetoric and logic followed by the *quadrivium* – arithmetic, geometry, music and astronomy before finally studying theology. Skelton delivered Henry's lessons in English which was a new concept being introduced by humanist tutors but his curriculum was not strictly a humanist one as he was not tutored extensively in Greek as during his childhood it had not yet become the highly popular subject it soon would be.

From the poem by Skelton, the references to 'Muses nine' and 'Helicon' indicate that Henry might have studied Greek mythology or at least began reading the ancient writings of Rome and Greece, although it is possible, he might have read translations of these in Latin or English. The nine muses being Calliope, Erato, Clio, Euterpe, Melpomeni, Thalia, Polymnia, Ourania and Terpischore that were appealed to by ancient writers for inspiration. It is apparent Henry studied Cicero *De Officiis*, as he added his name to his copy which also includes annotations by Henry and Skelton.[5] As a humanist Skelton more than likely did include Cicero in his curriculum for Henry as he himself had produced a translation of Cicero's *Letters* from Latin to English. *De Officiis* was one of the most renowned manuscripts to be rediscovered and became a standard piece studied during the Renaissance as part of a humanist curriculum studied by most who were taught Latin. *De Officiis* was a work on oratory and would be useful to those who might be faced with public speaking. Henry would of course also have to learn decorum and courtesy and Skelton used his own writings as part of his curriculum in teaching Henry, including *Speculum Principis* (Mirror for Princes). *Speculum Principis* was a guide to morality and virtue which Skelton presented to Henry in 1501 and from which Henry might have learnt a lot of his chivalric behaviour displayed later in life, although we know he certainly wasn't always the most chivalric man. The book encouraged Henry to have high regard for patrons of the arts who Skelton insisted were more valuable than the athletes the young prince probably admired based on his love of sport. Skelton condemned vanity and instead urged Henry to remain virtuous, emulating individuals such as Julius Caesar, Cato and Alexander the Great.[6] *Speculum Principis* (Mirror for Princes) is full of advice on the types of behaviour expected from a prince or nobility, both intellectually and in his private life. Amongst the advice are recommendations to study specific topics such as history and the choosing of a wife, as well as behaviours which ought to be avoided such as drunkenness and encourages Henry to honour and observe any oaths he might take.

Skelton was interested in mathematics and astronomy so it is possible his enthusiasm for these subjects was passed on to his eager pupil as Henry would later discuss astronomy with Thomas More. Unlike that of Arthur's, we do not have a reading list of Henry's but we do know Skelton likely used *Chronique de Reims* which narrates the third crusade and is written in French.[7] This might have been the book that inspired Henry's interest in military campaigns which he remained interested in throughout life.

William Blount, Lord Mountjoy, joined Henry's household as a companion to Henry in c.1499 until Henry reached fourteen years old when his formal education ended. Mountjoy's step-father was the chamberlain to Elizabeth of York and Mountjoy had a reputation of being a mature, well-educated young man who Elizabeth of York believed would be a good role model for the young prince. Although Henry at this point was still only a child, Mountjoy was in his early twenties and was to assist Henry with his learning as he himself had an admirable record of learning and had pursued his studies in Paris and continued to share Henry's lessons of Latin and history, which was a specific request of Henry VII. Henry would also learn games as well as courtly behaviour from Mountjoy through imitation. As an accomplished courtier, Mountjoy could role model the behaviours expected from Henry in a variety of activities; show Henry how to interact with ladies at entertainments, how to dress for specific functions, how to play the most popular card and dice games and gambling on the games so he hopefully would not lose too much money. Mountjoy had been tutored by the distinguished Desiderius

Erasmus and had arranged for Erasmus to visit Eltham Palace when he was in England. Mountjoy, Erasmus and Thomas More met with the royal children, Henry, Margaret, Mary and the infant Edmund during which Thomas More presented Henry with writings of Latin verse creating the beginnings of a long friendship which would end in Thomas More's execution. Having not been forewarned, Erasmus had not prepared a gift for the young prince and was embarrassed when Henry challenged him to present something. Erasmus followed this up by presenting Henry a ten-page Latin ode *Prosopopeia Britanniae* a few days later which was dedicated to Henry and his father and encouraged the prince to continue in his studies whilst advising that knowledge as well as being a patron of scholars was the path to fame. Erasmus also praised the skills of Skelton, 'I would add my exhortation to that end, were it not that you are of your own accord, as they say, underway with all sails set and have with you Skelton, that incomparable light and ornament of British Letters, who can not only kindle your studies, but bring them to a happy conclusion'.[8] Maybe this letter was partly the reason for Henry's keen learning even as an adult. Mountjoy was in the ideal position to pass on everything he had learnt from Erasmus which would undoubtedly influence Henry as a youth and as an adult. Mountjoy was not Henry's only companion, his schoolroom was shared with the sons of the aristocracy including Edward Neville and Charles Brandon, who would become Henry's closest lifelong friend and would marry Henry's sister Mary.

Upon the death of Henry's elder brother, Arthur on 2 April 1502, Henry's life changed as he became the heir to the throne at ten years old. The death of his elder brother was shortly followed by that of his mother, Elizabeth of York on 11 February 1503. Henry would also lose the head of his nursery, Elizabeth Denton, when she was replaced with male attendants. Henry was created Prince of Wales on 23 February 1504 and in June of the same year he left Eltham Palace to join the royal household in the company of his father. Henry's education on the art of kingship was now to begin but it contrasted greatly with the training Arthur had received when he was sent to Ludlow to learn to govern with the assistance of his own council. Henry was not sent to Ludlow but kept under the close supervision of his father and his apartments could only be reached through those of the king.[9] Henry was allowed to attend some functions with his father and possibly sat as a judge in the king's household but was not given such powers himself as Arthur had held in his teenage years and instead was to learn through imitation of his father. Writing to Queen Isabella of Castille, the Duke of Estrada stated:

> The Prince of Wales is with the King. Formerly the King did not like to take the Prince of Wales with him, in order not to interrupt his studies. It is quite wonderful how much the King likes the Prince of Wales. He has good reason to do so, for the Prince deserves all love. But it is not only from love that the King takes the Prince with him; he wishes to improve him. Certainly there could be no better school in the world than the society of such a father as Henry VII. He is so wise and so attentive to everything; nothing escapes his attention. There is no doubt the Prince has an excellent governor and steward in his father. If he lives ten years longer he will leave the Prince furnished with good habits, and with immense riches, and in as happy circumstances as man can be.[10]

Although this part of his education differed greatly from that of his brother it would have given Henry the opportunity to learn the role of the council, the different petitions he could be expected to preside over and also the roles of varying people at court.

Becoming heir to the throne also meant a change in Henry's education. Skelton was replaced by John Holt who aimed to tutor Henry in the liberal arts including grammar, logic, astronomy, theology of religion, music and geometry. Holt likely used his own book, a Latin grammar, *Lac Puerorum*, in his teaching of Henry. *Lac Puerorum* included diagrams to teach children the five declensions and explained technical terms in simple ways to make learning more fun for his readers.[11] Unfortunately, Holt's appointment ended with his death in 1504 and his fellow Oxford graduate William Hone was appointed in his stead. The accomplishment of his tutors as well as Henry's own abilities is evident in the fact that at age fifteen Henry wrote to Erasmus; he must have remembered the scholar from his visit as a child. Erasmus initially did not believe that Henry had been capable of such impressive Latin until it was confirmed by Mountjoy that the letter had indeed the work of Henry himself.[12]

Henry was enthusiastic about stories of chivalry such as the Arthurian legends featured in *Le Morte d'Arthur*, a popular title written by Sir Thomas Mallory and published by William Caxton in 1484. Another of Henry's preferences was tales of war, in particular the chronicles regaling the English victories of Henry V at Agincourt and Edward III at Crécy. These accounts would obviously remain with Henry as an adult as he sought recognition as a warrior king. These chronicles written by Jean Froissart and Jean le Bel were not available in English so Henry would have had to read them in French, indicating his fluency of French was way beyond that of a conversational standard but as king, he commissioned translations of the life of Henry V and Froissart's *Chronicles,* which told the history of the Hundred Year War in prose. The Flemish Giles Duwes (also spelt D'Ewes or Dewes) was responsible for Henry's study of French and based on his ability to read French books apparently was a good tutor, not only of French but also music as he also taught Henry to play various instruments. History remained an important part of the curriculum introduced by Skelton and it is likely Hone would have continued this with Henry, introducing him to the ancient historians such as Thucydides, Livy and Caesar's Commentaries and others which also featured in Arthur's curriculum as we shall see in Chapter Three, rather than English and French chronicles.

Mountjoy continued to read history with Henry even after his formal education came to an end indicating Henry's continued interest in the subject.

Music is known to have been a passion of Henry's and as a child, he learnt to play the virginals, lute, harpsichord, recorder and other wind instruments. Later his music tuition would be supervised and perfected by Duwes for his practice on stringed instruments and another tutor known as Guillam known as 'schoolmaster of pipes' for his playing of wind instruments.[13] Henry's sisters Margaret and Mary most likely shared his music lessons with Duwes and the siblings perhaps received lessons from the same dance master. The children could perform well at court when requested so the dance lessons must have been regular and effective. Henry would later partner Mary on a frequent basis at court entertainments indicating they enjoyed dancing together.

If Henry's curriculum under Holt and Hone followed the usual humanist favoured curriculum and one similar to his brother, then he likely continued to read classic Greek, translated to Latin and Roman writings of Aristotle, Plato, Vergil, Thucydides, Livy, Lorenzo Valla and Guarino of Verona but this list is only suggestive and by no means exhaustive.

Henry's formal education ended when he reached sixteen and at this point, he began to learn to joust, a pastime he came to both adore and excel at. Henry would practice running at the ring on a daily basis which was the training for jousting but he was not allowed to participate in any real tournaments due to now being the sole male heir over which Henry VII had become highly protective. Henry certainly made up for missing out once he was king. For martial sports Henry was taught archery and wrestling, as a proficient wrestler he even had a match with Francois I, King of France at the Field of Cloth of Gold in 1520 but embarrassingly for Henry, he was not the victor. The master of axes Thomas Simpson taught him to fight on foot with weapons including quarterstaff and poleaxes.[14]

Henry VII died 21 April 1509, aged fifty-two, and Henry VIII became king at seventeen years old. For the first few weeks of his reign, he was guided by his grandmother, Lady Margaret Beaufort. Henry VIII as a young king was prone to spending his days enjoying pastimes that were rather more enjoyable than dealing with affairs of state. Henry VIII was an eager sportsman and had learnt to hunt, hawk, play tennis, cast the bar and bowls before he ascended the throne. Henry VII also liked to hunt and hawk and likely spent time with Henry enjoying pastimes following the death of Arthur. When he became king, Henry VIII would hunt, joust, bowl and play tennis on a daily basis with his companions meaning someone else would have to pick up the real work. This person was to be Cardinal Thomas Wolsey who became invaluable to Henry VIII as he took on the burden of the majority of the work required at court whilst Henry VIII spent his days having fun. As he matured Henry VIII took a much more active role in the workings of his court and government.

Although his formal education had ended Henry VIII continued to study after his accession to the throne and he took a great interest in various subjects including medicine, topography and astronomy. He frequently spent time discussing and debating theological, astronomical and mathematical matters with Thomas More:

> and there some time in matters of astronomy, geometry, divinity and such other faculties and some time in his worldly affairs, to sit up and confer with him. And other whiles would he in the night have him up into the leads [the palace roof], there to consider with him the diversities, courses, motions and operations of the stars and planets.[15]

Henry VIII was a keen theologist and persisted in learning mathematics. His interest and capability in mathematics would help him to become an expert on fortifications and military planning and he also became very knowledgeable about maps and ships as he built up his navy. He kept a well-stocked library and even took a selection of books with him whenever he travelled. When Henry VIII acceded to the throne, Mountjoy encouraged Erasmus to return to England extolling the skills of the new king, telling Erasmus that the new king could speak fluent Latin, French and a little Italian and was accomplished with musical instruments.[16] It is possible Henry VIII might also have picked up some Spanish from his wife, Katharine of Aragon. Whilst he wasn't taught Greek as a child, Henry took it upon himself to learn the language as an adult and began taking lessons under the tutor Richard Croke. He also supported the spread of education, particularly the humanist curriculum and in 1540 he created five Regius Professorships at Cambridge; Divinity, Civil Law, Physic, Hebrew and Greek, ensuring the university was well stocked with humanists.

Henry VIII is one of the few English monarchs to have written a book. The authorship of the *Assertio septem sacramentorum* (Assertion of the Seven Sacraments), published as the work of Henry VIII in 1521, went through twenty editions in the sixteenth century. The work was a matter of speculation among the learned of Europe, and there were those who believed Erasmus had a hand in writing it but it is probably due to Henry's Latin style being influenced by the writings of Erasmus which Henry, as a youth, was no doubt encouraged to study and imitate by Mountjoy. While Erasmus would never deny that Henry might have had some help – 'since he has packed his court with men at once very learned and very eloquent' – he always acknowledged the quality of Henry's education and literary abilities: 'That prince possesses,' he wrote in September 1522, 'a wonderfully felicitous and apt mind, with which he is able to do remarkable things, whatever direction he turns it. Moreover, as a boy, he worked at improving his style, and that not indolently'. He went on to explain that there might be plausible reasons that Henry's writing had similarities to that of Erasmus himself; 'when he was a boy, he studied works of mine carefully, prompted to do so by the renowned lord William Mountjoy, a former student of mine, whom he was using as a study-companion at the time'.[17]

The Assertion of the Seven Sacraments was written against Martin Luther in defence of the Catholic doctrines of Mass. Theologians and scholars were summoned from Cambridge and Oxford to review the contents and the orthodoxy of the manuscript. Thomas More, renowned scholar and humanist, also reviewed the book. The title Defender of the Faith was bestowed on Henry VIII by Pope Leo X after this in 1521, a title Henry VIII was very proud of as an indication not only of his piety and loyalty to the Catholic church but also his intellectual abilities.

That Henry VIII was an accomplished young man cannot be denied, as reported by the Venetian ambassador Sebastian Giustinian:

> He is very accomplished, a good musician; composes well; is a most capital horseman; a fine jouster; speaks French, Latin and Spanish; hears three masses a day when he hunts, and sometimes five on other days. Attends the daily office in the Queen's chamber, consisting of vespers and compline. He is very fond indeed of hunting, and never takes this diversion without tiring eight or ten horses, which are stationed beforehand along the lines of the country he means to take. Before he gets home they are all exhausted. He is extremely fond of tennis, at which game it is the prettiest thing in the world to see him play, his fair skin glowing through a shirt of the finest texture.[18]

High praise indeed, but as ambassadors were often prone to flattery it is of no surprise that Henry VIII has been flattered so much after the ambassadors first visit to England.

As noted, Henry VIII adored music and as an adult enjoyed listening, playing and composing himself. As well as the instruments he was taught as a child he is known to have also played the organ and studied composition, composing from as early as eleven and later composing numerous works including *Pastyme with Good Companye* but did not compose *Greensleeves* as is sometimes stated. *Pastyme with Good Companye* became a favourite with all classes and was sung at court, in taverns and the streets of England, with its fun lyrics it is easy to see why:

> Pastime with good company
> I love and shall until I die
> Grudge who lust but none deny
> So God be pleased thus live will I
> For my pastance
> Hunt sing and dance
> My heart is set
> All goodly sport
> For my comfort
> Who shall me let?[19]

Henry VIII composed sacred, secular music and even a Mass and would perform his secular compositions at court to entertain his courtiers, he might also have had his choir perform his sacred compositions. He was an active participant in court plays and masques and would often entertain courtiers by singing solo or with a group. Henry VIII sought the most accomplished singers to join the Chapel Royal choir, even if this meant taking them from the choirs of his friends and would travel with a group of minstrels to entertain him. For musicians and composers, Henry VIII was the ideal monarch as he was keen to gather the best at his court and patronised many. As a youth, Henry had the perfect tutor to learn poetry in Skelton, who read the Latin poets with him as a child and as an adult, Henry VIII did compose English verse.

Although Arthur received a humanist education, due to his death, Henry VIII was the first English monarch to be taught under the influence of the Renaissance and the humanist favored curriculum. He would go on to become an accomplished Latinist, capable of composing tracts, statutes and music.

Chapter Two

Royal Children

Henry VII himself had spent a large portion of his early life in exile in Brittany. The details of his education are unclear but it is known he was pious, spoke fluent French and enjoyed considering financial problems. Bernard André, poet laureate, recorded the life of Henry VII in *Historia Regis Henrici Septimi* and states his tutor Master Andreas Scotus had reported Henry had a large capacity for learning, often surpassing his peers in his studies.[1] Henry VII's wife, Elizabeth of York, was versed in Latin, French and Spanish as her father, Edward IV, had instructed a tutor to teach Elizabeth of York and her sister Cecily in reading and writing.[2] Between them they had seven children, only three of which lived to adulthood; Henry, Margaret and Mary.

Henry VII came to the throne in 1485, at this time John Anwykyll was the headmaster of Magdalen College School, Oxford and he is thought to have been the first humanist schoolmaster. Humanism spread rapidly and it was not long before the Tudors were also influenced by its methods and ideas. Henry VII might not have been a renowned scholar himself but wished his children to receive the very best education. For this, he entrusted the education to scholars and professionals which, for the period was unprecedented, as royal children were usually taught by those of ecclesiastical careers and the nobility. Henry VII employed two kinds of tutors for his children; poet-orators and professional tutors, more of which will be discussed in Chapter Five. Henry VII did have a love of music, purchasing instruments to be played for him at court, which might be where his children acquired their love of music from, as all showed an interest in music. Henry VII was keen to patronise learning as was his mother Lady Margaret Beaufort who founded St. John's College,

Cambridge though this was done after her death by her executors as she had left a large sum for its building. She also refounded Christ's College, Cambridge. She was also the founder of the Lady Margaret Professorship of Divinity at both Cambridge and Oxford; it was initially a readership but is now a chair in New Testament and early Christian studies. Lady Margaret Beaufort was known to have been extremely pious so it is very easy to assume that all of her grandchildren would have been instructed from an early age in the Catholic faith and she was also likely involved in arrangements for the children's education and upbringing. All of the royal children would have been taught that the Pope is the head of the Church, appointed by God. For Margaret and Mary, their brother Henry would later become the head of the English Church. They would have learnt about participating in Mass, the Eucharist, transubstantiation and the miracle of bread and wine being turned to flesh and blood. They would have been taught what constituted sin was and the requirement for confession and repentance. Lady Margaret Beaufort was very charitable and this likely influenced the children too to believe in charity and good deeds, Mary in particular offered great support to those in her service and those she believed had just cause. With the exception of Arthur, very little evidence remains of the curriculum undertaken by the royal children but it can be inferred through their tutors and the few records available what the children possibly studied as the first royal siblings in England to receive a humanist education.

Arthur was the first child born to the Tudor monarchs on 20 September 1486 in Winchester. He was created Prince of Wales on 29 November 1489 at Westminster Hall, aged three. At this point he was also created Earl of Chester and Knight of the Bath; the bestowing of these titles suggested an end to Arthur's infancy and the beginning of his childhood. He had spent his early years mostly at the royal nursery at Farnham Palace and later Ashford, where he was cared for by those with close links to his mother, Elizabeth of York. The nurses were led by Elizabeth Tyrell, Lady Darcy, who had raised Elizabeth of York and her siblings. Elizabeth of York had two siblings who were still young at the time of Arthur's birth so it is likely she who arranged the attendants for Arthur, remembering those who had served her father, Edward IV.[3]

Whilst at Farnham Palace, Arthur would have learnt to ride from a very young age, horsemanship being a required skill for all noble-born and royalty. John Rede was appointed to begin Arthur's formal education when the prince was approximately five years old, although it is likely that by this point Arthur had already begun to learn to read and write. Under Rede, Arthur would begin his studies of grammar, Latin and French, although he would receive further tutoring in French from Giles Duwes around 1500 as he began to prepare for adulthood. By the time Duwes began to teach Arthur, he already had knowledge of French having been taught by Rede but he continued with his studies as French was seen as a required language of the wealthy.

André reports 'after achieving a swift and thorough knowledge of the first principles of literature, he was led through the finer points of the discipline by the best and most learned instructor, his teacher John Rede, with little effort on either part'.[4]

Arthur moved to Ludlow Castle as titular ruler of the Welsh Marches at the age of approximately six years old, to learn the art of kingship. Having received an interrupted education himself, Henry VII was keen to ensure his heir would be prepared when he succeeded his father to the throne. The idea of the royal heir making their base at Ludlow was practiced by Arthur's maternal grandfather, Edward IV, who had sent his son, Edward V, when he was a boy to learn to rule and this was a concept Henry VII was keen to implement and develop for his own heir. Arthur, as heir to the throne, was not brought up with his siblings and had a very different childhood. His education comprised of a classical education with physical training in addition to the skills required to become king. Arthur would study an excellent curriculum featuring humanist learning and authors but would also need to learn chivalry, manners and the legal jurisdictions under his rule, and how to work with other institutions such as the Church and courts. As well as learning to rule, Arthur would be required to learn the management of his estates for this would benefit him greatly not only as he matured and began to manage his own estates but also when he became king and would need to manage the realm. Through managing these estates, he would need to understand income, expenditure, titles, deeds and the people who worked and lived within these estates. These powers could be tested in the Welsh Marches where the heir, under the supervision of his council, could study the various documents that might come before him, practice his skill in presiding over people and events, and where his decision making could be monitored by his council without the possible widespread effects that could happen from decisions made in London. Arthur would spend time travelling the Welsh Marches, meeting his subjects and presiding over hearings and celebrations. His council and tutors would teach him the necessary behaviours, documents and proceedings as they went in order for him to earn through experience. By learning to rule from Ludlow the heir would be prepared to rule his kingdom when the time came. At an early age Arthur would begin to learn the lineages of the leading families and as with noble-born boys would also have to become familiar with the heraldry of the great families, by being able to recognise the symbols and arms of those families, including colours and badges. The arms would help to identify men on the battlefield but also help when presented in manuscripts and literature. The guidance of his counsellors would help Arthur put into practice the knowledge he gained from his academic studies, particularly the works studied under André. The skills he learnt in governing the Welsh Marches could also be put into practice when Arthur acted as regent during Henry VII's absence where he had the opportunity to observe the decision making of the government under the guidance of Henry VII's council.

Bernard André was appointed in 1496 when Arthur was ten years old, initially to assist Rede with Arthur's education but appears to have become the primary tutor and held his appointment for four years. André's recording of Henry VII's life is the reason we are aware of what Arthur studied and from the writings of André, it was likely him that introduced Arthur to humanist learning. André initiated a more humanist structured curriculum for Arthur and tasked him with the study of more challenging classical authors.

> I boldly assert this one thing, that though he was not yet sixteen years old he had either committed partly to memory or at least had turned the pages of or read on his own the following works: in grammar the writings of Guarino, Perotti, Pomponio Leto, Sulpizio, Aulus Gellius, and Valla; in poetry the works of Homer, Vergil, Lucan, Ovid, Silius, Plautus and Terence, in oratory Cicero's Duties, Letters and Paradoxes, and Quintilian; and in history Thucydides, Livy, Caesar's Commentaries, Suetonius, Tacitus, Pliny, Valerius Maximus, Sallust and Eusebius.[5]

From this list, we can gather that Arthur studied various works of humanist Latin grammarians and by the age of fifteen, had committed to memory either partly or in full the works of Guarino, Perotti, Pomponio, Leto, Sulpizio, Aulus Gellius and Valla, the Latin grammarians who were becoming popular at the time due to an increase in the New Learning. Of the grammarians, Gellius is probably the most famous, known for his *Attic Nights* which provides a compilation of notes on grammar, history, philosophy and other subjects. Lorenzo Valla was a fifteenth-century scholar who worked on improving the teaching of Latin grammar and rhetoric, his *Elegantiae Linguae Latinae* became one of the most prevalent works on grammar of the time along with Niccolo Perotti's *Rudimenta Grammaticae*. For his studies in oratory, Arthur studied Cicero, which would assist him in public speaking and understanding his moral duty. The works of Cicero were must-reads for anyone studying a humanist curriculum. *De Officiis* by Cicero is a philosophical treatise taking the form of a letter and highly recommended reading material for boys at the time, including

Arthur's nephew Edward a generation later. Arthur was gifted a copy of *De Officiis* by his grandmother Lady Margaret Beaufort who had it personalised to include an image of Arthur himself along with Tudor heraldry. Cicero's *Stoic Paradoxes* which is based on six famous stoic sayings also likely featured in Arthur's studies. Quintilian's *Institutes of Oratory* discussed the philosophical theories of Aristotle and were also memorised by Arthur in his study of rhetoric and oratory. Both of these works would assist Arthur in preparing speeches and structuring his point of view whilst also listening to alternative opinions and forming responses, key skills for a ruler.

Quite a few historians were included in the curriculum, mostly based on the Roman Empire and the numerous commanders. The historical works chosen by André for Arthur comprised of the popular commentaries by Julius Caesar detailing his war campaigns and Livy, a Roman historian who wrote the *History of Rome* which was studied by many including Machiavelli. Livy would be of particular importance due to the subject matter of individuals obtaining fame through their deeds, though this is likely to have been more popular with Arthur's younger brother, Henry. Valerius Maximus was a Latin writer and author of historical anecdotes during the reign of Tiberius (14 AD to 37 AD), Sallust, a Roman historian and politician, partisan of Julius Caesar, was one of the great Latin literary stylists noted for his narrative writings of political personalities, corruption and rivalry at court. Tacitus, a Roman historian and politician who wrote *Annals and the Histories* along with *Agricola's conquest of Britannia* discussed the Roman conquest and had a reputation for compactness of prose. Pliny the Elder, the Roman author and commander of the Roman army, was responsible for the encyclopedic *Naturalis Historia* which formed the basis for all future encyclopedias. Also included was Thucydides, an Athenian historian who wrote about the fifth-century war between Sparta and Athens, dissecting politics and war which was bound to enthral the minds of boys and young men. Suetonius, the Roman historian famous for his *De Vita Caesarum* (The Life of the Caesars), covered twelve Roman rulers including Julius Caesar and Nero. Eusebius was a scholar of biblical canon law, writing in approximately AD 300 and was a famed historian of Christianity. The reading of these works was not the extent of Arthur's education, he would be required to discuss and debate the works, to note specific details and show his understanding in both speech and writing. Some of the historical writings would also give Arthur insight into military campaigns and actions of the great leaders should he ever need to go to war but would also aid him in oratory skills and how a leader should act, the ideal reading material for an heir to the throne. Knowledge of military skills and commanding an army were vital for Arthur, as Prince of Wales he could command one of the largest forces in England if the need arose. Academic studies can only teach so much so it is likely members of his household also helped with understanding military campaigns.

This curriculum might seem very difficult for someone so young but it was not all strictly academic. Arthur also read poetry, although the authors he read were not easy reading and included the celebrated Greek poet Homer who wrote the *Illiad* and the *Odyssey*, both of which are viewed as some of the first writings in ancient Greek literature. André would write texts in the form of speeches or letters in Greek for Arthur to read and respond to pretending he was responding to foreign ambassadors or diplomats. Arthur's Latin poetry included the writings of Vergil, Ovid, Lucan and Silius, famous for his 12,000-line Latin poem covering seventeen books. Playwrights Plautus and Terence also featured in Arthur's reading. Arthur's copy of Vergil's *Aeneid* was published by William Caxton in 1498 and was dedicated to the prince. Arthur also practiced archery as is evident from Henry VII purchasing a longbow for him at the age of only five and he is known to have become a superb archer, he also owned armour and horses although there is no evidence of how accomplished he was in martial sports although Ludlow Castle did have a tiltyard so he might have practiced at the tilt when he wasn't busy with his academic studies and learning to rule.[6] Arthur was an accomplished dancer and likely would have learnt to play instruments whilst at Ludlow.

Unfortunately, none of Arthur's own work from his studies survives so we cannot know exactly how accomplished he was but can only accept André's praise of him that he was an intelligent and well-read. We do know Arthur was proficient in Latin as he exchanged letters in Latin with his future bride Katharine of Aragon. André himself also produced writings to aid Arthur in his studies including an index to his own commentary of *City of God* by St Augustine and from the list of works Arthur studied, it is apparent André took his duty seriously and sought out authors and topics that would provide Arthur with the most up-to-date, fashionable but overall useful curriculum to prepare him for his role as future king of England. With regards to his education, André likely had the biggest influence on Arthur and the works he chose for the young prince showed his knowledge in Renaissance learning and provided Arthur with the most innovative education of the time. The curriculum covered classic and modern writings making it the most comprehensive that could be provided. André ensured Arthur received the newest works but also included wisdom from the past.

Arthur's formal education is believed to have ended in 1500-1501 when he was preparing for his marriage to Katharine of Aragon but there is a record of an unnamed Scottish tutor whom nothing is known of, nor the curriculum he undertook with Arthur.[7] Aside from any tutor, Arthur would have continued to learn the art of ruling through his own household and council and that of Henry VII until his death at Ludlow Castle on 2 April 1502. Arthur was being formed into the model prince; intellectual, gracious and courteous.

Whilst Arthur was learning the art of kingship with his appointed tutors, his siblings were entrusted to their mother, Elizabeth of York. His younger brother Henry, elder sister, Margaret and younger sister, Mary were brought up mostly at Eltham Palace which held the royal nursery. The children were brought up together whilst Arthur missed out on any communal learning with his siblings. Elizabeth of York most likely taught all the children the basics in reading and writing herself as the handwriting of Margaret, Henry and Mary is all similar and is not the italic which was becoming popular in England. Being brought up amongst his sisters might have been an advantage to Henry which Arthur missed out on. Henry was clearly a confident child which might have stemmed from spending time with his sisters, we know Henry was confident enough to dance at court as a child, whipping off his doublet whilst we do not hear of Arthur behaving in this manner. However, this could also be the influence of the behaviours expected from Arthur as the heir and the responsibility he shouldered.

Margaret was born 29 November 1489 in Westminster Palace, the second child and eldest daughter of Henry VII and Elizabeth of York. Elizabeth Tyrell, Lady Darcy, was in charge of the royal nursery although she would have spent much of her time in Farnham with Arthur. Margaret was not yet two years old when Henry was born and began to share her nursery and although Margaret was the elder, Henry would have taken precedent over his sister as a male. The children would have had separate rooms and different attendants. It is likely Margaret and Mary were also taught to read and write by Elizabeth of York as both could read and write before the age of five. Margaret's education is little recorded but as with most girls at the time her daily life was probably organised according to a timetable of religious devotion, possibly prescribed by Lady Margaret Beaufort. Margaret and her siblings, once they joined her at Eltham, would likely start their day early by attending Matins before going to the chapel to hear Mass before they could enjoy breakfast. After breakfast lessons would begin and would last until dinner which at the time was around 11.00 am and was the main meal of the day during which appropriate material was likely read to the children. After dinner, there would be more lessons before again going to the chapel for Evensong. Supper would have been around 4.00 pm after which the children could enjoy pastimes of playing, singing, dancing or other alternative recreational activities before bed at 8.00 pm. The conduct of the royal children would have been watched at all times to ensure their manners were impeccable, even at mealtimes their behaviour and table manners would have been observed and corrected if their etiquette was not up to standard or they had not followed the usual protocols such as trying a little of everything offered rather than only one dish.

The Tudor princesses would have begun their education learning prayers and psalms and likely owned their own psalters and commonplace books. When Henry's lessons became more complex, his sisters, particularly Margaret due to the larger age difference between Henry and Mary, likely sat in some of his lessons, especially mathematics and Latin. As females they did not require the same level of depth and knowledge of these subjects as Henry, so would have only obtained an overview. The princesses would be required to know how to manage large estates including the servants and accounts, for this mathematics would be useful for managing their accounts and other topics would be beneficial in holding polite conversation at court. The princesses instead would focus more attention on needlework, and decorum as well as reading and writing, likely in the Renaissance italic which was becoming popular. Lady Darcy, Elizabeth of York or Lady Margaret Beaufort possibly instructed them in using herbs and plants from the garden for medicinal purposes and making tinctures and salves for their own use and their households. Music and dance would be an important aspect of the education Margaret and Mary received, as royal princesses they would be expected to dance and play instruments at court to entertain their parents, courtiers and ambassadors. Although it is apparent Henry was a very skilled musician, Margaret was also skilled and was accomplished in playing the clavichord and the lute, having likely shared Henry's lessons with Giles Duwes and she also had her own group of minstrels to play for and entertain the princess.[8] Another skill they would have learned from an early age was horse riding, Margaret actually became very accomplished at hunting whilst, although Mary was an accomplished rider, we do not know if she enjoyed the hunt as much as her siblings.

Margaret also learned French from Giles Duwes before she left England to become Queen consort of Scotland following her marriage to James IV of Scotland. It was actually Margaret's husband, who, in 1496, would decree the first compulsory education act in Europe when he made it compulsory for sons of landowners in Scotland to attend school.[9] When betrothed at the age of ten, Margaret would have undertaken the learning of etiquette and how she should act not only as a princess but as a queen. Margaret had the perfect tutors for this in the form of her mother Elizabeth of York and her grandmother Lady Margaret Beaufort. In 1503 Margaret left England to travel to Scotland, aged only fourteen she was accompanied by Lady Surrey who would act as both companion and mentor to the young queen consort. As with Arthur, Margaret would need to learn the art of ruling as she would become regent of Scotland from 1513 to 1515. As consort Margaret would not have needed as much knowledge so it is likely she had much assistance from her council to learn how to govern. Of all the children of Henry VII, it seems Margaret was the least scholarly and has been referred to in more recent times as a princess who 'was neither a learned nor an educated princess'.[10]

Mary was born 18 March 1496 at Sheen Palace and was the fifth child born to Henry VII and Elizabeth of York and the fourth to survive infancy.[11] At six years old Mary received her own household supervised by Elizabeth Denton, including her own schoolmaster who was appointed due to the age difference between Mary and the two siblings she shared Eltham Palace with. Mary's education consisted of Latin, music, dance and embroidery although it is likely her governess taught her the latter. In music, Mary could play the lute, clavichord, and the virginals and was often called upon to entertain guests at court. Prince Philip and Juana of Castile visited the English court in 1506 and Mary was called upon to entertain the guests by playing the lute and clavichord and later dancing for which she received praise for her skills.[12] Mary was betrothed to Charles of Austria, who would later become the Holy Roman Emperor, Charles V, in 1507 and having been taught by her sister-in-law Katharine of Aragon, she sang songs in Spanish at the courtly celebrations of the betrothal. Whether Mary persisted with studying Spanish isn't known, nor do we know if she understood the songs or if Katharine had just taught her by rote. Either way, to be able to sing songs at a court celebration in Spanish at such a young age is impressive, even though the marriage did not go ahead. Mary was also instructed in French by Giles Duwes and had Jane Poppincourt; a French companion, allocated to her when she was five years old. Jane was placed in Mary's household both as a companion and to assist Mary in learning conversational French. John Palsgrave was later appointed in 1512 to teach Mary French in a more formal manner. The lessons and companionship would later serve her well when aged eighteen, she married Louis XII of France and became queen, taking Palsgrave with her when she travelled to France. Mary was known as a beautiful princess who excelled at dancing, 'deportment in dancing is as pleasing as you would desire'.[13] Sharing a household, the sisters had ample opportunities to practice their dancing and music together and it is imagined that Henry might have also joined in the fun.

John Skelton was appointed in the 1490s and had impressive credentials after studying abroad and was a member of the close circle of early humanists in England. He was a man bursting with ideas, humour, languages and verse. Although appointed directly as tutor to Henry it is likely Margaret and Mary benefitted from his appointment and were probably instructed in grammar and handwriting practice by Skelton along with Henry although it is likely his tutoring of Mary was at a lower standard due to her age. As the siblings handwriting is similar, it is likely that Elizabeth of York taught them initially but they all went on to practice under Skelton even though Skelton's writing differs to that of the royal children. Mary also shared William Hone with Henry but again it is highly likely the two siblings were taught at different levels due to the age gap and gender. When Henry's formal education ended around 1509 Hone continued in royal service as tutor to Mary. Little is known about the curriculum Mary received under Hone but as he was an accomplished Latinist it could be assumed he taught her Latin and grammar. Although at the time Latin was not seen as an important part of education for girls it is feasible that both Margaret and Mary learnt Latin as it remained the language of the Church and no doubt their pious grandmother would urge them to be able to understand the scriptures. Mary was also encouraged to persist with her Latin studies by her sister-in-law, Katharine of Aragon.

Giles Duwes taught all of Henry VII's children, firstly music, in particular the lute and later French if required. The children's grandmother Lady Margaret Beaufort was a patron of learning and known to have been extremely pious so it is possible Margaret and Mary found instruction under her or least followed a curriculum agreed with her. Mary spent time at her grandmother's house who is known to have read books in French, this would have provided Mary with further opportunity to practice her French speaking and reading.[14]

It is evident all of the royal children received an excellent education, but that of the princesses was much less academic and strenuous than either of the brothers, as expected for the period and not as accomplished as that their nieces, Mary and Elizabeth, would receive a generation later. Residing in the same household as their brother Henry certainly provided a benefit to the sisters in that they were able to take advantage of the tutoring of some of the most renowned tutors of the time. It appears Mary might have been more intellectually intrigued than her elder sister Margaret. The Tudor princesses were the first royal females to undertake a humanist-based curriculum and whilst it was not as extensive as that of their brothers it was impressive for girls at the time and certainly more thorough than could be expected of other females, in particular those of the lower classes.

Chapter Three

All the King's Children

As a king of high intellect, Henry VIII wished to ensure his children received an education to match their status. All of Henry VIII's children would be taught to ride from an early age as physical exercise was deemed important to education. They would also be taught deportment, languages and etiquette amongst other subjects. Regardless of the fact they were children of the king, they all had to learn how to show deference to adults and in particular their father. The boys would be taught to bow and for their father, this would include going down on one knee as Henry had done himself to his own father. The girls would be taught an elegant curtsey in which they would keep their back straight, eyes lowered and hands would have to be placed perfectly as they lowered into a curtsey. Henry VIII's own education had been of a humanist curriculum and he surrounded himself with those of the 'New Learning' which becomes evident in the tutors he chose to appoint for his own children.

Mary was born 18 February 1516 at Greenwich Palace to Katharine of Aragon and would become Mary I of England. Katharine of Aragon would have liked to have educated her daughter herself but royal protocol regulated that, following the christening, a child would be handed to the royal nursery under the supervision of a lady mistress. The honour of this appointment went to Elizabeth Denton who had been the lady mistress of Henry VIII as a boy. Elizabeth Denton was replaced in 1518 by Margaret, Lady Bryan, mother of Sir Francis Bryan also known as the Vicar of Hell, but this was to last only a short time until 1519 when she was replaced by one of Mary's godmothers, Margaret Pole, Countess of Salisbury.[1] Margaret Pole was the daughter of the ill-fated George, Duke of Clarence, alleged to have been drowned in a barrel of Malmsey wine as his punishment for treason, and brother to Henry VIII's grandfather, Edward IV. Margaret Pole was also cousin to Henry VIII's mother Elizabeth of York, so it is likely Henry VIII knew her well. Margaret Pole had married Sir Richard Pole, lord chamberlain to Prince Arthur. Jane, Lady Calthorpe, replaced Margaret Pole in 1521, but Margaret Pole would remain a prominent figure in Mary's life.

Mary's education began early and in 1517 she was presented with her first primer by the Duchess of Norfolk.[2] The primer was a small book that would have contained all the religious texts a child was expected to learn by memory, the Lord's Prayer, Ave Maria, Creed and the Ten Commandments. Under the supervision of Margaret Pole, Mary had begun to learn to read, starting with her ABC and then learning vowels and letters, building up to sounding out words. As with children today, pictures were helpful to children learning and books with woodcut pictures were used for the same purpose in the sixteenth century. As a princess, Mary had to learn courtly etiquette as well as singing and dancing but also received instruction in more academic subjects including languages, religious instruction and the classics. Mary excelled at music and by the age of four could play the virginals and would later learn the lute and regal.[3] It is likely to have been Margaret Pole who taught Mary to play the virginals as she had been a keen musician herself with an excellent education but Mary was later to receive a professional music tutor in the form of Philip van Wilder, the favourite musician of Henry VIII who frequently played for Henry VIII in his privy chamber.

Although it cannot be confirmed, due to the timeframe and the style of writing, which was based on the traditional style rather than the newer italic font, popular with Renaissance scholars and tutors, it is likely to have been Margaret Pole who taught Mary to write. As a wealthy child, Mary would have learnt to write with a quill rather than slate, although she might have used slate at the beginning. Despite Mary having a lady mistress, Katharine of Aragon maintained an active interest in Mary's education and began to teach her Latin, French and Spanish. Katharine of Aragon herself had received the best education available as her mother Isabella of Castile had employed two humanist tutors to assist her in educating her daughters. Katharine of Aragon was literate in Latin and used the language to correspond with Arthur before she left Spain for England. Katharine of Aragon was evidently keen to ensure her daughter also received the best possible education. Unlike her siblings, there is no evidence that Mary shared her schoolroom even though this was recommended, this does not mean she did not have study companions, it is just unfortunate we do not know if she did or who they might have been.

Mary was not given the practical education in government she would have received if she were a boy, despite her being the heir to the throne. England, unlike France, did not have a law preventing the accession of a female heir, therefore, there is no reason Mary could not reign other than the Tudor belief that females were the weaker sex, mentally inferior and were subject to their husband's authority, meaning if Mary married, her husband would rule, rather than Mary. Katharine of Aragon's mother Queen Isabella of Castile had ruled in her own right so Katharine of Aragon did not see a problem with Mary reigning. Henry VIII did instruct male tutors to provide Mary with a comprehensive Renaissance education which aimed not only to instruct her in the discharge of her public duties in the future but also to build her character to reach the best of her potential. This education was dominated by the Spanish scholar Juan Luis Vives. Vives had been retained by Katharine of Aragon in 1523 to draft an educational plan for Mary, the result being *De Ratione Studii Puerilis* (On the right method of instruction for children). The tract included recommended reading for boys and girls. Mary's curriculum was heavily influenced by religion as Vives recommended study of the Bible and reading the New Testament daily as well as writings of theologians St Augustine and St Jerome. Vives preference for character building is prevalent in the recommended reading which was based on authors who encouraged living well as well as cultivating knowledge. Those who purely aimed to instil knowledge were omitted from the reading which included orators, poets and historians.

Vives had previously written *De Institutione Feminae Christianae* (The Education of a Christian Woman) dedicated to Katharine of Aragon and containing a wealth of advice on preserving Mary's virtue and encouraging her morality. The work contains a full chapter based on women ranging from historical females of ancient Greece through to Katharine of Aragon and her sisters. The accomplished daughters of Sir Thomas More are also mentioned by Vives as he believed their impeccable virtue had been improved through their studies of religion and improved their conduct. History was included in Mary's studies in the form of introducing Mary to historical females who she could emulate, Catherine of Alexandria and Catherine of Siena were both saints whilst Cassandra and Chryseis were both priestesses of Apollo and Juno.[4]

Vives himself never acted as tutor to Mary but it is apparent the programme of study created by Vives was not ignored and might have provided the curriculum used by her tutors. The syllabus instructed Mary to grasp the eight parts of speech: noun, pronoun, verb, adjective, adverb, preposition, conjunction and interjection and the five declensions of Latin; nominative, vocative, accusative, genitive, dative and ablative. Once understood, Mary could then begin translating English into Latin, first small verses and gradually advancing to more comprehensive works. Mary was instructed to take notes of any words, phrases and writings she found interesting in a notebook known as a commonplace book. According to Vives, Latin should be learnt to be used in conversation and through the use of the vernacular. Vives also provided Mary with a reading list that encouraged only moral behaviour and was urged to avoid romances that he thought were distracting and did not instil moral behaviour in females. This did not mean Mary did not enjoy reading material other than academic works but instead, she was encouraged to read stories of virtuous women. The reading list recommended by Vives included the classical works of Cicero, Plato, Seneca, Boethius, Demosthenes and Tertullian as well as modern works by Erasmus and More, which although impressive differed to reading recommended by Vives for boys.[5]

Aged nine, Mary was sent to Ludlow where Margaret Pole was recalled to her service, to continue her education and preside over the Council of Wales and the Marches in her role as Princess of Wales even though this title had not been formally bestowed upon her. Mary was accompanied by councillors, attendants and her first recorded appointed tutor, Dr Richard Fetherstone, who would support her in her new role and continue her education. Katharine of Aragon appears grateful that Mary has finally been appointed a tutor as nine years old was late for a royal child to be appointed a tutor, this usually occurred at the age of six or seven.

Mary could already speak and write Latin at this age and was encouraged to continue her studies of Latin and French but also to persist with her music lessons, practising the virginals and spinet. Fetherstone was a devoted Catholic and it is likely he made religion central to Mary's education and by eleven years old, Mary was capable of translating a Latin prayer into English. Giles Duwes, an experienced French tutor, was appointed to improve Mary's French. Duwes accompanied Mary to Ludlow with his large collection of musical instruments and books which Mary had access to and could practice her music. As with learning Latin, Mary would have begun learning French by pronouncing the letters, nouns, pronouns, verbs and adverbs before moving on to converse by learning texts by rote. Once Mary could converse, she would be tasked with writing mock letters and short pieces based on well-known and familiar topics before progressing on to more difficult texts, first learning them by heart then reading from them in French. This is of course if she followed the guidance of Duwes in his French grammar *An Introductory for to Learn to Read, to Pronounce and to Speak French Truly.*[6] Little is known about Mary's ability in other languages although it is believed that as well as Latin and French, she could speak Italian and possibly Spanish, no doubt due to the influence of her mother, Katharine of Aragon. It is known that Mary was never provided with a Greek tutor unlike her half-brother Henry Fitzroy but this does not mean she did not learn it at all. Mary's education at Ludlow was not restricted to formal education, she was also to learn deportment, dancing and managing her household which was perceived as important for girls, especially for those who might have the responsibility of running large estates when they matured.

Mary's skill in translation can be inferred by the fact in 1545 aged twenty-nine she translated Erasmus's *Paraphrase on the Gospel of John* under the encouragement of Katharyn Parr. Mary's health left her unable to complete the translation but it was published in 1546 with the final elements completed by another. Mary indeed was intellectual but it is apparent her education differed to that of her siblings.

Henry Fitzroy, born 15 June 1519 at the Priory of St Lawrence in Essex, was Henry VIII's first son to survive infancy. He was the son of Henry VIII's mistress, Elizabeth Blount. Henry VIII acknowledged Fitzroy as his son, 'Fitzroy' literally meaning son of the king but as he was not the son of Henry VIII's queen Katharine of Aragon, he was illegitimate. Cardinal Thomas Wolsey stood as the boy's godfather and would remain an important part of Fitzroy's life, often acting as a go-between between Fitzroy and his father. When replaced by Margaret Pole as lady mistress of Mary, Lady Bryan was charged with the supervision of Fitzroy.

Fitzroy was made Duke of Richmond and Somerset and was established in his own household at Sheriff Hutton and was expected to support himself from the income gained from his estates and revenues, unlike Mary who was maintained by their father. He had a small council to initiate him into the workings of the government and politics. Fitzroy's first official tutor was the renowned scholar,

John Palsgrave, although it is thought Fitzroy received an elementary education in Latin from an unknown monk. John Palsgrave had experience of teaching royal children as he had previously taught Henry VIII's sister, Mary and was a close friend of Sir Thomas More. Fitzroy was to learn Latin and French for which Palsgrave, having devised simpler methods of teaching French and Latin, was more than qualified for the task. To begin Fitzroy's education of Greek, Palsgrave chose a comedy by Plautus in the hopes it would provide entertaining learning for his young charge. Once accomplished in the basics, Fitzroy read Latin and Greek grammar before beginning to read Latin poetry and classical authors including Virgil's *Eclogues* and writing short essays based on his reading.[7] Fitzroy was not the studious type and Palsgrave requested assistance, which Cardinal Thomas Wolsey responded to by providing an assistant whose role would also be to tutor Fitzroy in singing and music.[8] Palsgrave did not have an easy task in tutoring Fitzroy, who preferred to spend his time on more leisurely activities. As Palsgrave was uncomfortable using corporal punishment to encourage his pupil, he attempted to try and motivate him by adding companions to the schoolroom, a common occurrence in wealthy households. The companions were mixed according to social status and age, including nobility, gentry and Fitzroy's family members, but this proved a mistake as the companions often distracted Fitzroy from his studies and demeaned Palsgrave by allegedly taunting him and undermining his authority. In an effort to make lessons more enjoyable for the boy and therefore encourage his participation, Palsgrave requested a painter to illustrate the lessons, prompting Henry VIII that 'It is a great furtherance in learning to know the names of things by their pictures'.[9] He also shortened the lessons to help with the child's short attention span but it was all in vain. Unfortunately for Palsgrave, the painter was not provided, having been retained by Henry VIII and instead Palsgrave was only to receive an assistant. Religion was not omitted from Fitzroy's studies and he was brought up with similar learnings to that of Mary rather than the more evangelical teachings received later by Elizabeth and Edward. Fitzroy is not reported to have been staunchly Catholic and there is no evidence of how he felt about the Reformation or the dissolution of the monasteries, unlike Mary who we know was vehemently against it and remained a devoted Catholic all her life.

Palsgrave was replaced in 1526 by Richard Croke through Cardinal Thomas Wolsey's intervention. Unfortunately, Croke faced the same problem as Palsgrave and found it difficult to focus Fitzroy on his studies. In a torrent of complaints to Cardinal Thomas Wolsey, Croke complained that Fitzroy has fallen under the bad influence of Sir George Cotton, a gentleman usher in the duke's household. Fitzroy spent his time with his companions hunting, hawking and practising archery at the butts, often missing his lessons or arriving so late he was too tired to study, putting at risk the curriculum Cardinal Thomas Wolsey had planned for his godson. Cotton also disrespected the position of Croke and would taunt him in the schoolroom, defending Fitzroy and his failures in his studies. Cotton even went as far as completely undermining the teachings of Croke who had been teaching Fitzroy to write in the favoured italic by attempting to teach him to instead write in the traditional cursive font.[10] Cotton was not the only person Croke had problems with, Sir William Parr, Fitzroy's uncle and chamberlain, also took it upon himself to change the schedule by arranging for Fitzroy to attend matins and vespers at the time he was due to attend lessons. Like Palsgrave, Croke was reluctant to use physical punishment, possibly for fear of reprisal. It is not known what Henry VIII's thoughts were on these matters but thankfully Croke eventually succeeded and gained control of Fitzroy by agreeing on a more interesting curriculum. Rather than studying poetry and philosophy, Fitzroy was to turn his attention to the books of *Julius Caesar* and the Gallic Wars. For a young boy, these works were exciting, full of battles and war and finally captured his young mind and encouraged him to learn. His interest in the subject is made clear in a letter to Henry VIII the next year where he 'requests a harness for his exercise in arms, according to his learning in Julius Caesar, in which he hopes to prosper as well as he has done in other learnings'.[11] Fitzroy followed this letter with another to his godfather, Cardinal Thomas Wolsey, advising him he had made a request to his father and asking him to support his request. Croke was replaced in October 1527 and left Fitzroy a much more educated young boy than he had found him. It is not certain who replaced Croke as Fitzroy's accounts only refer to him as 'a new schoolmaster' but it is possible this might have been George Folbury who had recently returned from studying divinity in Montpellier. Fortunately, there was no further cause for complaint regarding Fitzroy's studying so it is possible Croke had succeeded in turning him into a scholar, albeit initially a reluctant one, leaving Folbury with a much easier role until Fitzroy was approximately twelve years old when his formal education ended.

Fitzroy's education might appear to be all academic but this is not the case. In the true Renaissance style, he was also taught to dance along with the popular pursuits of riding, hunting and shooting with the longbow and possibly also running at the ring in the hopes of making him a successful jouster like his father, famed for his skill at the joust. It also took a more mature turn and Fitzroy attended parliament aged ten years old, no doubt an attempt to educate him on proceedings for participation in the future. Fitzroy returned to court in the early 1530s, making Windsor his base, accompanied by Folbury and was provided with a companion in Henry Howard, Earl of Surrey. Surrey was a couple of years older than Fitzroy but was apparently a brilliant scholar as well as skilled in martial sports, making him the ideal role model for Fitzroy. The pair studied together but also partook in pastimes and even held mock tournaments. In 1532, aged thirteen, Fitzroy was sent to France with Surrey with the aim of improving his French and visiting the French court to develop his courtly manners and behaviour. Fitzroy returned to England in 1533 to continue learning about the machineries of government and was married aged fourteen to his companion's sister, Mary Howard. Unfortunately, Fitzroy died on 23 July 1536, still in his teenage years, leaving Henry VIII without a male heir once more.

Elizabeth, the future Elizabeth I, was born 7 September 1533 at Greenwich Palace to Anne Boleyn. At only a few months old Elizabeth was sent to Hatfield under the care of her nurse. Lady Bryan was appointed as Elizabeth's governess but was replaced in 1537 by Blanche Herbert, Lady Troy. Another gentlewoman appointed was Katherine Champernowne (later known as Kat Ashley) and was to become a prominent influence in Elizabeth's life along with the niece of Lady Troy, Blanche Parry. Aged nine, Elizabeth joined her younger brother Edward's household but it was not until she reached the age of eleven that Elizabeth received her first official tutor, John Picton. Prior to this, she had been taught by Kat Champernowne to the best of her ability, although it is likely she was receiving tutoring from an unofficial source, possibly a gentleman within her household. Elizabeth is renowned for her intellectual skill and could apparently sew by the age of six. Champernowne was well educated for a female at the time and allegedly instructed Elizabeth in French, Italian and Spanish along with her native language, Welsh. Whilst in the same household as Edward, Elizabeth benefitted from being able to share his tutors and likely came to the notice of Edward's tutor, John Cheke, for her intellect as it was Cheke who called William Grindal to court to become Elizabeth's tutor.

William Grindal, appointed in 1544, was the first to introduce Elizabeth to a humanist curriculum including Latin and Greek, a subject her sister Mary had not had the opportunity to study. Elizabeth had already begun studying Italian under John Picton and continued to progress under the supervision of Giovanni Battista Castiglione, a distant relation of the famed author Baldassare Castiglione who wrote *Il Cortigiano* (The Book of the Courtier). Later, Elizabeth would continue to share more of Edward's tutors including John Belmaine with whom she learnt French and Roger Ascham who would teach both children to write in the modern italic hand, a style he had mastered as did Elizabeth as evidenced from her flamboyant swirling signature. Elizabeth was fond of working on translations, translating poems and other well-known works into various languages. When she was eleven years old, she translated the eleven pages of French in *Le Miroir de l'âme pécheresse* (The Mirror of the Sinful Soul) written by the French king's sister, Marguerite of Navarre. A year later, Elizabeth would excel in her translating with Katheryn Parr's *Prayers and Meditations* which she translated into French, Italian and Latin at only twelve years old. Elizabeth presented her translation as a gift to her father, Henry VIII. Roger Ascham replaced Grindal in 1548 following the latter's death and likely influenced not only Elizabeth's studies in Latin and Greek but also her religious beliefs. Under Ascham, Elizabeth progressed her double translations using the works of classical writers, Demosthenes, Isocrates and Tully, and would practice daily until she mastered both Latin and Greek.

Unlike Mary, Elizabeth was introduced to the writings of classical authors that Vives had not recommended including Livy, Sophocles, Isocrates, and other classical rhetoric works. When Elizabeth had mastered the easier classical authors, Ascham challenged her further with the orations of Demosthenes and Æschines in an effort to teach her the art of eloquence and public speaking.[12] From Ascham's book *The Scholemaster* we can get an idea of Elizabeth's studies. *The Scholemaster* is split into two books; the first on bringing up youths whilst the second focuses on mastering Latin. In the first book, Ascham discusses the works of Cicero, Tully, Horace, Terence, and Socrates as authors for all scholars but also recommends particular authors for specific topics. For philosophy he suggests Plato, Aristotle, Xenophon, Euclide and Theophrast whilst for eloquence and civil law his recommended authors are Demosthenes, Æschines, Lycurgus, Dinarchus, Demades, Isocrates, Isæus, Lysias, Antisthenes and Andocides. Both Grindal and Ascham would have instructed Elizabeth in history, possibly using Ascham's recommended authors of Herodotus, Thucydides and Xenophon.

Whilst we know Elizabeth studied some of the authors recommended by Ascham, it is possible she might have studied them all and most assuredly would have learnt from Cicero the four cardinal virtues expected of a prince; prudence, justice, temperance and courage. Lastly, Ascham provides recommended poets; Æschylus, Sophocles, Euripides and Aristophanes.[13] In the second book Ascham expands on the aforementioned authors to master the Latin language and adds Quintilian, Caesar, Dionysius, Pliny the Younger and Pliny the Elder and notes the art of double translation and specifically Elizabeth's skill in completing translations.[14]

As an adult Elizabeth was fluent in Greek, Italian, Latin and French and was renowned for her literary skills, often noting incorrect words or phrases laid down by her ministers in court documents. As queen, Elizabeth continued to enjoy reading history, setting aside several hours each day purely for that purpose, she also continued to complete translations and frequently wrote prayers and poems along with letters in various languages, she translated Boethius's *The Consolation of Philosophy* in 1593 showing she continued to undertake these tasks all her life. Ascham would engage his royal pupil in debates on the classic authors which in turn assisted her in improving her skills of rhetoric and logic.

Elizabeth's love of music and dancing is well known so it is of no surprise to know that she was taught to play instruments and dance as a child and became a skilled performer of the lute and virginals and continued to practice regularly even once queen. As a girl, she would have minstrels and players to entertain her and likely continued the habit of being read to or entertained by music during mealtimes. Elizabeth did not spend all her time in the classroom and was fond of riding and blood sports such as hunting and cockfighting. No doubt Ascham joined her in these pastimes as he was fond of sports, even writing on the subject of archery.

Edward, born 12 October 1537 at Hampton Court Palace to Jane Seymour, was the long-awaited legitimate male heir to the throne and would become Edward VI. Lady Bryan found herself transferred from Elizabeth's household to the appointment of Edward's governess. He spent his first few years raised by women who had the responsibility of teaching Edward the fundamentals of etiquette. More formal instruction would have been provided by dance masters who would have taught Edward how to walk, sit and stand in postures befitting his rank as a royal prince and heir to the throne. His chamberlain, Sir William Sidney, and his steward, Sir John Cornwalleys, were tasked with ensuring Edward was brought up as a Renaissance prince. Edward's first tutor was to be Richard Cox, a severe disciplinarian, appointed when Edward was approximately six years old. Before his first tutor was even appointed, Henry was already thinking about Edward's education. In 1538, Henry was building Nonsuch Palace and had decorative panels installed, these panels would provide an education in image form, depicting figures from history, mythology and legend.[15]

A child's sixth birthday was a major milestone for the Tudor's as it marked the end of infancy. For Edward this meant, in July 1544, his household changed, his female attendants were replaced by men and his second tutor, John Cheke, was appointed. Edward is the only Tudor monarch that we know of to have kept a diary, which he began aged nine or ten and he recorded his birth along with significant milestones in his chronicle, writing:

> Afterward [he] was brought up, [un]til he came to six years old, among the women. At the sixth year of his age he was brought up in learning by Mr. Dr. [Richard] Cox, who was after[ward] his Almoner, and John Cheke, (Bachelor of Arts crossed out) Master of Arts, two well-learned men, who sought to bring him up in learning of tongues, of the scripture, of philosophy, and all liberal sciences. Also John Belmaine, [a] Frenchman, did teach him the French language.[16]

Edward would begin his formal education in the same manner as many boys, with Latin grammar using the approved Latin grammar textbook produced by William Lily. Edward was apparently a keen student and mastered his grammar but also was obedient and respectful of his tutors, thanking them for pointing out his faults. Of the two tutors, Cox was the strictest whilst, Cheke, preferred to encourage his pupils rather than instil fear through threats of beatings. His tutors had to maintain a balance of teaching Edward to obey and show deference to his elders, in particular his father, but also to rule, which he was expected to do as the heir to the throne whilst remaining virtuous and displaying the moral behaviours and education of a true Renaissance prince. Like all boys of noble birth Edward would be required to learn the lineage of the nobility and their arms. Cheke likely used images for this to assist Edward in recalling names, faces and coat of arms.[17]

Edward's education followed a humanist curriculum known as *bonae litterae* championed by Erasmus. The curriculum focused on Latin and Greek grammar and once Edward had mastered the basics of Latin grammar, he moved on to more difficult works. Rhetoric, study of the scriptures and classical authors formed part of Edward's curriculum with reading based on Cato and Aesop. Cheke was clearly an effective tutor as by the age of eight Edward had memorised four books of the Roman grammarian and poet Publius Valerius Cato and was effectively writing in Latin, quite an achievement for an eight year old. At around the same time he was reading Aesop's *Fables*, Edward also began to compose letters which he would write in his own notebook in an effort to improve not only his handwriting but also his grammatical composition. The use of a notebook to practice grammar and handwriting exercises was a popular method amongst children and even adults kept notebooks of their favourite quotes or poems. Edward learnt to write using a quill and ink and developed his writing in the popular Renaissance style of italic. Some of these letters remain to this day and show Edward to have been an eager boy, respectful but also very formal for one so young.

As with his siblings, religion formed part of Edward's curriculum and he would read from the Old Testament and proverbs on a daily basis. It is apparent Edward enjoyed poetry as he quoted the Latin poet Cato in his letters and would later go on to read the poetry of Horace.[18] The *Distichs of Cato* were short pieces to help Edward learn Latin and instil morality and virtue. Edward shared his schoolroom with fourteen boys, the sons of noblemen and his father's favourites, all of a similar age to Edward. Amongst the boys were Henry, Lord Hastings, Robert Dudley, and Barnaby Fitzpatrick. The sons of Charles Brandon, Duke of Suffolk, Henry and Charles Brandon were also his companions and Henry's doodles are present in the schoolwork of Edward.[19] Unlike Fitzroy, Edward's companions do not appear to have distracted him from his studies and proved able study companions, although that is not to say Edward was always well behaved and Cox had threatened to beat the prince. Cheke's curriculum included the method of double translation, the boys were tasked with memorising passages of Latin, first translating them into English and then back again into Latin. Works by Erasmus and Vives were not absent from Edward's reading and between 1546 and 1549 he and his companions had advanced to the Latin writings of Cicero, Livy and Lucian as well as Greek authors such as Herodotus, Aristotle, Plato and Isocrates. In 1550, regarding Edward's intellectual abilities, Ascham wrote:

> Our King's ability equals his fortune, and his goodness surpasses both;- or rather, as it becomes a Christian man to speak, such is the manifold grace of God, that in eagerness for the best literature, in pursuit of the most perfect religion, in willingness, in judgement and in perseverance – that quality you most value in study, he wonderfully exceeds his years. In scarce of any other particular do I esteem him more fortunate than that he obtained John Cheke as the instructor of his youth in sound learning and true religion. Latin he understands

with accuracy, speaks with propriety, writes with facility, combined with judgement. In Greek he has learned the Dialectic of Aristotle, and now learns his Ethic. He has proceeded so far in that language, that he readily translates the Latin of Cicero's Philosophia into Greek … He will shortly finish the Ethic, which will be followed by the Rhetoric of Aristotle.[20]

Edward studied Euclid's *Elements,* a treatise made up of thirteen books of mathematics, which might have spurred Edward's interests in mathematics. Robert Recorde's *The Pathway to Knowledge (1551)* was the earliest English work on geometry and formed part of Edward's reading.

History was a subject favoured by humanists and was therefore included in Edward's studies. The works of Pliny the Younger include letters, one of which was an account of the eruption of Mount Vesuvius in 79 AD which destroyed Roman cities and killed his uncle Pliny the Elder, and were most likely read by Edward along with Plutarch's *Parallel Lives,* containing biographies of famous Greeks and Romans. Thucydides *History of the Peloponnesian War,* an account of the war between Sparta and Athens in fifth century BC was most assuredly included as it was for most boys undertaking a humanist curriculum. Geography likely featured in Edward's studies, as a future king he would be required to learn the locations of all other relevant kingdoms as well as the landscapes and oceans.

As heir to the throne, Edward had the additional burden of learning to rule. For this, Cheke selected the writings of Cicero, *De Officiis.* Cicero had been a Roman orator and politician and was recommended reading for all noble boys at the time. The works of Cicero had been incredibly popular as one of the manuscripts commissioned to be copied once it had been discovered and its study became an integral part of humanist education. Cheke enlisted the assistance of Roger Ascham, famed for his skill in penmanship, to develop Edward's handwriting. The work of Giovanni Batista Palatino was used for this purpose as Edward progressed through the models in his notebook, improving his handwriting as he went. This practice taught Edward precision and to pay attention to detail which might have been how his chronicle began, as a way to record details he had noticed or wished to remember. Either way it was likely started as another exercise set by his diligent tutors.

Languages were not ignored and Edward began to learn French before his tenth birthday, tutored by Cheke's nephew, Jean Belmaine, who had also taught Elizabeth French. Nine years old might seem very young to us for a child to be learning Latin and French but this was expected at the time especially of a royal child. Edward's study of French was extremely competent and he studied the dialogues of Pierre Du Ploiche who produced a phrasebook including everyday conversations but also prayers. Edward did not cease his French studies at being able to converse but continued to the point he was writing essays in the language based on religion including his faith, the Catholic faith and idolatry, clearly showing at a young age that his religious leanings were not towards the Catholic faith. Edward's study of languages would continue for the remainder of his life. Edward's tutors favoured the Protestant religion so it is possible that their influence resulted in Edward's faith.

As a royal prince, Edward's curriculum was wider than that of most boys although it is not known if additional subjects such as mathematics and astronomy were taught as part of his curriculum or if Edward himself decided to study them. Henry VIII was a keen student of astronomy so it might have been through his father's influence that Edward came to be interested in the subject and collect astronomical instruments. Despite the strict academic curriculum, Edward was not restricted to the schoolroom and was also taught to dance, fence, ride and play musical instruments, including the lute which he was taught by Philip van Wilder, a favourite musician of Henry VIII. As a child John Ashley (married to Kat Champernowne) had begun teaching Edward to play the virginals. Various musicians were employed to entertain Edward when he had acceded to the throne, his love of entertainment and music made clear as well as the fact that he had been known to actively partake in masques himself as well as presenting Greek and Latin orations to the court on a regular basis. Edward was keen on physical sports partaking in hawking, hunting, owning greyhounds and horses for these pastimes, and he also enjoyed archery. Roger Ascham presented Edward with his own book on archery, *Toxophilius* in 1545, after which Edward became highly skilled at the sport.[21] Some of these sports aimed to instil martial education as did his participation of riding at the tilt. His more leisurely sports consisted of fishing, tennis and hawking, owning his own hawking gloves and fishing rods even as a young prince. As Edward matured and his studies intensified, he was given his own study which we know contained his own personal writing desk covered in black velvet with an embroidered 'E' but also another desk contained his writing tools and instruments. Edward was provided with all he needed to study; paper, knives to trim his quills, tables of slate for writing, along with mathematical and astronomical instruments; wooden compass, scales and weights.[22]

Henry VIII died 28 January 1547 and Edward succeeded him to the throne at just nine years old. Too young to rule himself, a council was arranged to rule in his stead. In 1549, two years into his reign, Edward's education changed again. Six counsellors were appointed by the Duke of Northumberland to attend Edward and continue his education. The purpose of this was to ensure Edward was learning how to rule and being kept up to date with the activities of the Privy Council while he remained a minor. It was at this time that Edward began to spend more time on physical pursuits, riding at the tiltyard and learning the use of weapons.[23]

Sir John Cheke ensured Edward remained studious as his formal education continued to the age of fourteen at which point he was able to recite all the English ports as well as those in Scotland and France as part of his studies on his kingdom and those closest. It is believed it was Cheke who encouraged Edward to keep a journal which still survives and provides insight into Edward's daily activities. In 1552, Edward's formal education ended after eight years of laborious study of Latin and Greek. This did not mean he ceased learning but instead began to learn statecraft under the direction of William Thomas who introduced him to state papers and set him exercises of drafting mock state papers and agendas which Edward excelled at and also enjoyed. As with his sisters, Edward also completed translations, largely verses from the English Bible into French.[24] Although it appears Edward's education was difficult and intense, he still had time to enjoy learning more fun activities such as hunting and jousting.

It is apparent all of Henry VIII's children received an excellent education and the best that could be offered at the time. It might seem that Mary's education is lacking in comparison to that of her siblings but it was common for more detailed records to be kept of boys than for girls at the time and with regards to Elizabeth, much of her achievements are known through the records of her tutors and herself so it is possible that Mary was not as boastful as her sister and therefore her educational achievements less known. All of the siblings apparently enjoyed music which becomes obvious in the courts of Edward, Mary and Elizabeth who regularly held entertainments, pageants and masques. The royal children also appear to have excelled in languages, particularly Elizabeth who continued to complete translations for fun once she became queen. It is also apparent they learnt deference from an early age and mastered the art of politics and hiding their feelings which would be of benefit to those who would eventually reign. The education of the royal children would provide the standard for other children, especially those of the aristocracy who would seek to emulate the curriculum and would also use private tutors where affordable. All of the royal children benefitted from tutors who at the time were renowned for their intellect but it was not just their personal tutors who influenced education in England under the Tudors.

Chapter Four

Tutors of the Tudors

During the Tudor era, there were very few female teachers, those who did teach tended to be petty school teachers and were likely to be a wealthy widow who had allowed a room in her home to be used as a schoolroom. Some scholars did argue for female tutors but this was not deemed to be appropriate by the majority.

Throughout the period even following the Reformation, education and religion were tightly bound, often the family priest was the tutor to children where it could be afforded. Many schools were run by the Church as parish priests were bound to provide education to parish children. It was also accepted that parish clerks could teach the children of their parish but there remained a lack of tutors in some areas of the country. Chantries, which were chapels founded by the wealthy, often had schools attached. With the dissolution of the monasteries, many schools were closed or refounded on secular lines but religion remained fundamental to education. With the increase in humanistic teaching and the introduction of the printing press, many tutors produced didactic works to aid students in their studies. It would be impossible to discuss all the tutors of the times but in this chapter, I have sought to include those who were responsible for teaching royalty or who had a recognisable impact on education either through their teaching or the writings they produced to aid studies, some of these tutors and their works are still very well known today.

Although not a tutor to the royal family, John Stanbridge influenced many of those who would go on to become royal tutors or brilliant scholars. Stanbridge was educated at Winchester and New College where he received his Master of Arts. He had been usher under John Anwykyll and became master of Magdalen College School upon

Anwykyll's death in 1488. Stanbridge was later master of Banbury School and was largely responsible for the revision of many Latin texts used in Tudor schools. He aimed to provide a more humanist influence in his revisions, which proved popular and were published frequently. He is thought to have composed and printed at least six works of his own including *Parvula*, *Accidence* and *Vulgaria*, all with the principle aim of improving speech, grammar and helping children with translation exercises. Some of Stanbridge's works took the form of sentences in English with their Latin translation and others included Questions and Answers to assist children in their understanding of translations and composition of sentences. Stanbridge was working at the same time the printing presses were beginning to prove popular so was one of the first to have his work shared on a wide basis throughout the Tudor schools. Stanbridge either studied with or tutored men who would become the most renowned in their field for the era, some of which will be discussed in more detail.[1]

The leading scholar of the day was Desiderius Erasmus, born in Rotterdam on 28 October 1466. In 1475, Erasmus was sent to a Latin school with his brother. The school also offered Greek lessons, something not usually found below university level and this is where Erasmus first became interested in the language. Erasmus left the school in 1483 when his parents died of plague. In 1487, Erasmus became a canon at St Augustine and was ordained in 1492. Some of his later works argue for the reformation of the Church due to abuses within and it is thought he witnessed these abuses during his time as a priest. Pope Leo X issued a dispensation shortly after, allowing Erasmus to accept a post as secretary to the Bishop of Cambrai. By this time Erasmus had already gained a reputation as a man skilled in Latin. The Bishop of Cambrai agreed for Erasmus to enrol at the University of Paris which was already being influenced by humanism in 1495.

Erasmus first visited England in 1499 and taught at Oxford and came to be friends with Thomas More and John Colet, Dean of St Paul's. These men shared the opinion that to understand the scriptures, the study of classical languages and literature was of vital importance. Erasmus believed that the scriptures were the true Word of God and to read and understand them in their original form was the guide to morality and religion. Whilst Erasmus was supportive of church reform he was and remained a Catholic. Colet and Erasmus both wished to improve education and when St Paul's School was founded by Colet in 1510, Erasmus gave his support to the school even compiling a textbook for its use and was a champion of female education.[2] Erasmus was such a keen scholar that whilst in England he learnt Greek by studying it avidly for three years which would enable him to study theology on a more philosophical level. Erasmus was one of the predominant humanists whose life's work was to produce a modern Greek edition of the Bible amongst other writings, this was influenced by the rediscovery of Valla's *New Testament Notes* which inspired Erasmus to continue with his studies of the New Testament eventually producing a translation in Greek and Latin. He would later argue that the sixteenth-century pronunciation of Greek was incorrect in terms of some consonants and the use of diphthongs. Erasmus' pronunciation of Greek was used in Cambridge until in 1542, Stephen Gardiner, chancellor of the university, forbade its use and issued an order that any undergraduate using Erasmus' version would be whipped only for his version to be reinstated under Elizabeth I.[3] Erasmus graduated a Doctor of Divinity from the University of Turin in 1506, later lecturing at Leuven before returning to England. Whilst in England he stayed with Thomas More and the two scholars idled their time away translating the works of poet Lucian from Greek to Latin. The translation was printed in 1506 and proved to be highly popular.

The person responsible for bringing Erasmus back to England and to teach at Cambridge in 1511 was John Fisher, Bishop of Rochester and chancellor of the university. Fisher was the first to hold the position of The Lady Margaret Professor of Theology at Cambridge, a position founded by Lady Margaret Beaufort. Fisher sought to bring a humanist curriculum to England and make Cambridge relevant on the European map of educational establishments and he did just that when he succeeded in recruiting Erasmus to teach Greek and theology in the position of Lady Margaret Professor of Theology from 1511-1515, especially as at that time there was no official position of a Greek lecturer at the university and would not be one until a few years later. Fisher himself began to learn Greek when he was over fifty years old, whether he was taught by Erasmus isn't known but it is possible. Erasmus later refused to spend the rest of his career at the university instead preferring to be able to continue with his own studies and writings. He had a number of patrons including William Blount and William Warham who was studying at Oxford at the same time John Rede was enrolled. Rede would later become tutor to Arthur whilst Warham would patronise Erasmus having both been influenced by the New Learning present at New College. Erasmus was a pioneering Latin stylist who preferred the new more relaxed style of Latin than the older extravagant Latin favoured in the fifteenth century.

Amongst the works produced by Erasmus are the Greek New Testament and a Latin New Testament for which he used all the vulgate manuscripts he could obtain in order to create his versions. Along with these he also produced a number of didactic works including *Institutio principis Christiani* (Education of a Christian Prince) and assisted Colet with the production of Greek textbooks for use at St Paul's School. His religious works such as *Sileni Alcibiadis* resulted in criticism as he remained faithful to the papal authorities but did wish to see reform. Due to this, some reformists wished him to take further steps and become Protestant which he was not willing to do, on the other side Catholic's criticised him for critiquing the Church. The works of Erasmus became widespread and his followers became known as Erasmians. Erasmus was part of a circle of humanist scholars including Colet, Thomas More, William Latimer, William Grocyn, Thomas Linacre and Richard Pace. These men promoted the study of Greek and Latin, produced books, writings and would shape the future of education in England as well as serve Henry VIII as he surrounded himself with humanist scholars. Humanists sought to study the ancient texts, recover their true meaning and give readers the opportunity to interpret doctrine themselves. Whilst Erasmus might not have tutored Henry VIII directly, he certainly contributed to his education indirectly through his tutoring of William Blount.

William Blount, 4th Baron Mountjoy, was technically not a tutor but served as a companion and role model to Henry. It was also Mountjoy who introduced Henry to Erasmus who played a huge role in education during the Tudor era. Mountjoy initially studied at Cambridge under Ralph Whitford before travelling abroad with his tutor to continue his studies. Whilst in Paris the pair met Erasmus, who resided with them tutoring Mountjoy in rhetoric and Latin. On returning to England in 1499, Mountjoy invited the scholar to accompany him. Mountjoy arranged for a visit at Eltham Palace with himself, Erasmus and Thomas More. Thomas More had prepared Latin writing for Henry but as Erasmus had not been warned he had come unprepared. The young Henry challenged Erasmus on the lack of writing and Erasmus, in turn, wrote a ten-page work named *Prosopopoeia Britanniae Maioris* praising Henry and his family. Through his influence on Mountjoy, Erasmus certainly influenced the education of Henry VIII who undoubtedly understood the value of learning by the time he inherited the throne. Mountjoy and Erasmus both preferred the new easy style of Latin rather than the older more elaborate Latin, through their influence Henry grew to prefer the new style too unlike his first tutor, Skelton. When Henry reached fourteen, Mountjoy was appointed as Lieutenant of Hammes Castle in Calais but he mostly remained at court attending Henry on a daily basis, continuing Henry's study of Latin and encouraging him in his correspondence. Mountjoy was the epitome of the noble courtier, learned, gracious but also partook in courtly pastimes of hunting and dancing, making him the ideal courtier to act as a role model to the young prince.

Prominent in Erasmus' circle was John Colet who had studied abroad, largely in Florence where he had become interested in the New Learning. On his return to England, he introduced the New Learning to Oxford by lecturing on the Pauline epistles, before being appointed as the Dean of St Paul's in 1503. Colet used his knowledge when delivering his sermons, influencing all social ranks to believe that learning was essential, in particular the study of the scriptures and their interpretations. Colet was influential at court where he delivered the Good Friday sermon for a number of years during the reign of Henry VIII. A considerably wealthy man, he used his fortune to found St Paul's School in 1509 and set out the regulations that 153 boys should be taught at the school free of charge. There is no doubt that Colet was keen to provide an education for all classes and this education would include religion as its primary focus. Colet enlisted his circle of friends to assist with the foundation of St Paul's. Erasmus was not the only one to help with this as Richard Pace also wrote a handbook on rhetoric for the school and would go on to publish translations of the Greek writings on rhetoric by Lucian and the philosophy of Plutarch. Colet himself published a treatise on accidence, *Aeditio*, for the school and wrote the statutes for the school himself. St Paul's was to incorporate a full humanist curriculum consisting of classical authors and modern authors including that of his friend Erasmus.

Known as one of the most learned men of his time, John Rede was a professional pedagogue and was esteemed within the scholarly circle at Oxford and made connections with scholars and churchmen. Rede had attended Winchester College and enrolled at New College, Oxford in 1472, receiving his Bachelor of Arts in 1477 and his Masters in approximately 1480. He was a fellow of New College, Oxford between 1474-1484 but vacated the fellowship to accept the position of headmaster of Winchester School until he was appointed as the tutor of Arthur in approximately 1491. Rede returned to Winchester College again in 1501 where he remained as warden until 1520 when he returned to New College as warden, a position he held until his death in 1521.

Rede was replaced or at least joined by Bernard André in 1496 and retained a role in the royal household, possibly remaining as a joint tutor until 1500 at which point André was given the opportunity to commence his work *Vita Henrici Septimi* (The Life of Henry the Seventh).[4] Bernard André was a blind Augustinian friar originally from Toulouse. He had been installed as poet laureate in 1485, three years before Skelton received his first laureateship. Before being appointed as tutor to Arthur he had already gained a reputation for his skill in composing Latin verse and had taught at Oxford University. Arthur's education under André was certainly humanist and thanks to André we have the best record available to gain an understanding of what the Tudors studied. André had initially been appointed to assist Rede who he wrote was 'the best and most excellent teacher.'[5] André was a dedicated tutor who wrote didactic works specifically for his student. Unfortunately only one of these survives, the aforementioned index on André's commentary of *City of God* written in 1500. When Arthur married, André found himself in the role of the royal historiographer and is the author of *The Life of Henry the Seventh,* a valuable if somewhat possibly biased biography of Henry VII's life. During his time as historiographer André also acted as an orator compiling a number of public speeches and poems for state occasions for Henry VII and Henry VIII until his death in 1522.

John Skelton replaced André as poet laureate and was tutor to Henry VIII. He first met Henry VII in 1488 when the king was visiting Oxford University where Skelton was studying rhetoric after having previously studied at Cambridge. Henry VII conferred a laureateship in classical Latin rhetoric on Skelton. This was a degree that had never before been awarded in England so was a high honour. Skelton had previously served Elizabeth, Countess of Surrey, but after coming to the attention of Lady Margaret Beaufort soon found himself invited to the royal court to join the likes of the Gigli brothers writing poems for the royal family. He was then appointed as tutor to Henry c.1496. During his appointment, he wrote *Speculum Principis* for Henry, a guide on how the young prince should behave. Following his admission to holy orders two years later he became Henry's chaplain. Skelton received high praise from the renowned Desiderius Erasmus, who described Skelton as 'a light and glory of English letters'.[6] Skelton produced a number of works including *Speculum Principis*, the book on behaviour he had presented to Henry in 1501 and a series of satirical works based on society and life at court known as *The Bowge of Court*. He also wrote plays and was the playwright of *Magnificence*, a play which was performed at the court of Henry VIII. As poet laureate, he wrote speeches for Henry VIII and also poems of English military victories. He also wrote a number of mocking pieces about Cardinal Thomas Wolsey including *Speke Parrott* and *Colin Clout* which, fortunately, did not harm his career as Wolsey later became a patron of Skelton.[7]

Skelton was talented in languages and wrote poetry in English, Latin and French. *The Garlande or Chapelet of Laurell* was printed in 1523 and is a 1600-line humanist favoured poem of an autobiographical nature. The poem refers to Skelton himself in the third person, and he takes the opportunity to praise his own works and accomplishments as poet laureate and tutor to Henry. As talented as he was, it is of no surprise he found himself to be worthy of such a poem. The title itself refers to the ancient tradition of poets being crowned with a garland of laurel. It dates back to ancient Greece where poets would compete and the winner was crowned, the laurel being sacred to Apollo, the god of poetry but the tradition had been lost. The tradition had been re-established during the Renaissance in 1341 with the crowning of Petrarch in Rome. Skelton himself had been crowned an unusual three times between 1488 and 1493, at Oxford, Louvain and Cambridge. Henry VII bestowed the 1488 laureateship and also gifted Skelton Tudor livery with 'Calliope' embroidered, Calliope being the Muse of eloquence and poetry.[8] A laureateship was deemed to be the equivalent of an advanced degree and although Skelton was a skilled poet he was also accomplished in the scholarly study of Latin and rhetoric. *The Garlande or Chapelet of Laurell* provides insight into the instructional works created by Skelton:

Of your orator and poet laureate
Of England, his works here they begin:
In primis the Book of Honourous Estate;
Item, the Book how men shoulde flee sin;
Item, Royal Demeanance worship to win;
Item, the Book to speak well or be still;
Item, to learn you to die when ye will;

Of Virtue also the sovereign interlude;
The Book of the Rosier; Prince Arthur's Creation;
The False Faith that now goeth, which daily is renewed;
Item, his Dialogues of Imagination;
Item, Antomedon of Love's Meditation;
Item, New Grammar in English compiled;
Item, Bowge of Court, where Dread was beguiled;

His comedy, Achademios called by name;
Of Tully's Familiars the translation;
Item, Good Advisement, that brainless doth blame;
The Recule against Gaguin of the French nation;
Item, the Popinjay, that hath in commendation
Ladies and gentlewomen such as deserved,
And such as be counterfeits they be reserved;

And of Sovereignty a noble pamphlet;
And of Magnificence a notable matter,
How Counterfeit Countenance of the new jet
With Crafty Conveyance doth smatter and flatter,

And Cloaked Collusion is brought in to clatter
With Courtly Abusion; who printeth it well in mind
Much doubleness of the world therein he may find[9]

Although these verses include plays and poetry produced by Skelton, we know that he also produced several didactic works. The first verse appears to be translations or books guiding on courtesy and morality. Skelton also makes reference to a Latin grammar to assist children in learning Latin which might have been used by Henry. The reference to Tully's *Familiars* is a translation of Cicero's *Letters*, a work which we know Arthur, Henry and Edward all studied. These verses form only a small part of *The Garlande or Chapelet of Laurell*, the full poem includes much more. After Skelton was replaced as Henry's tutor, he was appointed rector of Diss which he held until his death in 1513 but Henry clearly held his old tutor in high regard as he appointed him orator regius in 1512 making him an advisor and poet to the king.

John Holt replaced Skelton around 1502 when Henry became heir to the throne. He was a professional innovative Latin tutor who was part of the humanist circle with Thomas More and Erasmus. Holt was educated first at Magdalen College School before attending Magdalen College, Oxford and in 1490 became a junior fellow of Waynflete's foundation of Magdalen College, specialising in Latin, receiving his Master of Arts in 1494. Holt progressed to become assistant master or usher of Magdalen College under the headmaster John Stanbridge, where he taught for two years before being employed in Cardinal Morton's household at Lambeth Palace as tutor to the boys there around 1496. It was during his time at Lambeth Palace that Holt wrote *Lac Puerorum* (Schoolboys' Milk), a textbook for schoolboys on Latin grammar, compiled with woodcut illustrations to help children remember their Latin and of which Thomas More wrote the introduction.[10] As Thomas More wrote the introduction and concluding epigrams to *Lac Puerorum*, it is likely Holt was not only interested in humanism for his own studies but also for his teaching of children.

The work includes recommended reading for boys which Thomas More expands on by encouraging students to also read the works of grammarians Giovanni Sulpizio, Perotti, Siponto and Diomedes.[11] Holt was appointed headmaster of Chichester School in 1501 but within the next year or so was appointed as Henry's tutor, an appointment that would last no more than two years due to his death in 1504.

Holt was replaced by William Hone upon his death. Hone had also graduated from Magdalen College, Oxford, obtaining a Bachelor of Arts in Theology, and had been a demi at Magdalen College School between 1496-97. Hone was another who was present under the headmaster John Stanbridge, before becoming a fellow at All Souls College, Oxford between 1498-1503. Like his predecessor, Hone also taught in Cardinal Morton's household and at Chichester School. Hone taught not only Henry but also his younger sister, Mary and was named as schoolmaster in plans of her travel to Calais to marry the future Charles V.[12] Unfortunately, it is unclear when Hone ceased tutoring Henry and began to teach Mary, they might have shared some lessons, but we do know he was Mary's tutor by 1508 so it is possible at this point Henry's formal education came to an end so Hone was transferred to the household of Mary. John Palsgrave was appointed to tutor Mary in 1513 but it is unclear whether this was to supplement or replace Hone. After this point Hone is recorded as royal chaplain until 1514-1515 but there are no records of a royal appointment after this and he died in 1522.

William Lily was appointed by John Colet as the first High Master of St Paul's school. He had studied in Rhodes and became one of the first Greek scholars in England by 1500. Lily was a demi at Magdalen College School in 1486, the same time Holt, Grocyn and Wolsey were involved with the school and was the author of Lily's grammar. It was authorised for use in most schools for many years by Henry VIII and had become known as the Royal Grammar. Whilst appointed at St Paul's, Lily composed two books; *Rudimenta* and *De Constructione*. Both were written to teach syntax and Erasmus reviewed the latter before it was published in 1513. Lily's son George would later publish a series based on the English humanists.[13] It is from this tract that the suggestion that Thomas Linacre was a tutor of Arthur possibly originates due to a translation of Linacre's that was dedicated to Arthur.

Linacre was another famed humanist scholar who studied at Oxford before travelling to Florence to continue his studies, amongst his fellow students was Giovanni de' Medici who would later become Pope Leo X. Linacre then travelled to Padua to study medicine. On returning from studying abroad in 1499, he tried to gain an appointment as tutor to Arthur, possibly by presenting his translation of Proclus to Henry VII, but was seemingly undermined by André and was unsuccessful in his aim to tutor Arthur. Linacre did later succeed in obtaining a royal appointment when he was appointed as royal physician to Henry VIII in 1509 and later supervised the studies of Henry VIII's daughter Mary. He was also one of the first English scholars to study Greek and is renowned for translating the Greek physician and philosopher, Galen's works into English from Greek and Latin. Linacre was part of a group of educated men that petitioned Henry VIII for the establishment of the Royal College of Physicians which was granted in 1518 with Linacre as its president.[14]

John Palsgrave was appointed as tutor to Mary, sister of Henry VIII in 1512 and would later travel to France with her in 1514 as her secretary but by late 1516 he was studying law in Louvain. He was a Renaissance scholar and was later appointed as tutor to Fitzroy. Palsgrave graduated with a Bachelor of Arts from Cambridge in 1504 and also received his Master of Arts from the University of Paris, he completed his education with a degree in theology at Oxford in 1532. He was fluent in various languages including Latin, Greek and French. Palsgrave was the author of a Latin play and had created a new approach to learning French producing his French and English dictionary and grammar titled *Lesclarcissement de la Langue Francoyse*. The French grammar was approved for all grammar schools by Henry VIII. Palsgrave was part of the scholarly circle of friends of Erasmus and Thomas More.

The only tutor to teach all Henry and all of his siblings was Giles Duwes, a Fleming accomplished in French and a lutenist. Duwes appears to have initially been appointed as a musician in the household of Henry VII but was later appointed around 1500 as tutor to Arthur and would later tutor Henry, his sisters Margaret and Mary, and lastly, Henry's daughter, Mary. Duwes taught French to the children and also taught at least Henry and possibly his siblings, to play the lute from 1501. As well as an apparent successful tutor, Duwes also published a French grammar; *An Introductory for to Learn, to Read, to Pronounce and to Speak French Truly* initially written in the 1520s but not published until 1533 and was the result of his experience as a royal tutor, the work being dedicated to Henry's daughter, Mary. The work was esteemed for its advice on pronunciation and provided readers with example letters along with a selection of useful words, grammar and conversational exercises for students to memorise. The book comprises French passages with English translations and even poems written by Duwes for the book. When Henry VIII ascended the throne Duwes was appointed as Henry VIII's librarian so he must have been held in great esteem by his past pupil, who recruited Duwes' son, Arthur, firstly as a lute player and later as a tutor to Fitzroy.[15] In 1521, he published his alchemical treatise *Dialogus inter naturam et filium philosophiae* which was translated from Latin to English after his death. Duwes was still in service as Mary's tutor when he died in 1535. Other than Duwes, the tutors selected by Henry VII for his children all favoured a humanist education. That these tutors and scholars such as Erasmus influenced Henry is clear in the choice of tutors he chose for his own children, beginning with Juan Luis Vives.

Juan Luis Vives was born in Valencia c.1492 and began his education in Valencia where he was apparently taught to compose tracts against the New Learning during his scholasticism studies. He left Spain around the age of seventeen and enrolled at the University of Paris to continue his education. It was whilst in Paris that Vives began to favour the New Learning which he had previously written against. On leaving Paris, Vives secured the appointment as a tutor to a noble boy, Guillaume de Croy and spent the next few years with his pupil. In 1519, whilst lecturing at Louvain, he wrote a tract in favour of the New Learning which might have resulted in his appointment as a professor at the University of Louvain. During his time in Louvain, he was noted by Erasmus and later made the acquaintance of Sir Thomas More in 1521, a friendship that would continue through the exchange of scholarly correspondence and friendly competition. Thomas More, impressed with the scholar praised him to Erasmus who responded 'I rejoice that my estimate of Vives agrees with yours. He is one of the number of those who will overshadow the name of Erasmus'.[16] Thomas More would also recommend Vives to Katharine of Aragon who became a patron of his. In 1522, Vives wrote his *Commentaries* on Saint Augustine's *Civitas Dei* (City of God) and dedicated it to Henry VIII as well as dedicating his moral tract *De Institutione Feminae Christianae* (The Education of a Christian Woman) to Katharine of Aragon. The next year, Vives was retained by Katharine of Aragon to write an educational plan for her daughter Mary. Vives provided *De Ratione studii puerils* (On the Right Method of Instruction for Children) in 1523, this resulted in Vives being noted by Cardinal Thomas Wolsey who installed him at Corpus Christi College, Oxford to teach rhetoric. Vives clearly made an impact on Henry VIII and Katharine of Aragon as he was awarded a royal pension but this would end when years later, he was imprisoned for supporting Katharine of Aragon against Henry VIII in the annulment of their marriage. He was released after six weeks and left England shortly after, returning to Bruges where he died in 1540.

Vives believed in the education of females and was likely the first to write a book specifically on the education of girls. His most influential works were those previously mentioned along with *De subventione pauperum* (On Aid for the Poor) and *De trandendis disciplinis* (On the Subjects of Study). Although Vives advocated the education of females he also thought the education of girls should differ from that of boys due to the female role in society and that their reading should be limited and should not include romantic works. Vives provided a very thorough reading list, for boys and girls only the Christian poets were the same and consisted of; Aratus the Greek didactic poet, Juvencus, Paulinus, Prosper of Aquitaine who was the first to continue Jerome's *Universal Chronicle*, Prudentius and Sidonius Apollinaris. For pagan poets, Vives suggested Lucan, Seneca and Horace for girls, with Virgil, composer of three of the most famous Latin poems; *Eclogues*, *Georgics* and *Aenid*, and Italicus as additional texts for boys. For history, girls were encouraged to read the work of the Roman Florus, Justinus, the Latin writer, and Valerius Maximus whose works could also provide instruction in morality. Boys were encouraged to study Julius Caesar, Plutarch who was known for *Parallel Lives*, his biographies of famous Greeks and Romans, Sallust, Seutonius, Thucydides who was renowned for his account of the Peloponnesian War between Sparta and Athens, and Xenophon. Models of composition for both boys and girls focused on Cicero but other than that they differed with girls being urged to read Seneca, Plutarch and Plato, the teacher of Aristotle and boys were encouraged to read Terence, Erasmus and Pliny. After this, the subjects differ with girls being encouraged to read moral writings of St Ambrose, St Jerome, St Augustine, Erasmus and Thomas More along with the New Testament. Vives also gave a list of sources of interesting stories for girls; Lucretia in Livy which is the story of how Lucretia's suicide might have sparked the Roman Empire, Griselda known for her virtue, Praetextatus and Joseph in the Bible. Boys were instead tasked with the study of philosophy and the works of Plato and his student Aristotle. Other recommendations included Theophrastus along with tracts based on agriculture by Cato, who recommended farming for its security and advised on resource management, Columella's *De Re Rustica* discussed ploughing and cultivation, Pallidius, Vitruvius, Varro and Pliny, who was the chief source on Roman gardens, discussed crop rotation and horticultural species.[17]

Vives was also very strict in that he did not think it appropriate for a lady to dance or attend tournaments at court which during the Tudor era was near impossible if a lady wished to secure a husband and find favour for her family. One of the most influential statements made by Vives was that education was the responsibility of the state, schools should be established in every town and funded by the authorities with guilds taking some responsibility. This would create a much more consistent approach to schools across the country. Vives wished to improve teacher training and methods of education and believed teachers should understand their pupils to enable them to improve the quality of their own teaching. By 1546, his works had been translated into multiple languages and had been published numerous times. Vives is probably, alongside Erasmus, one of the most influential innovators of education. Some of his recommendations remain in practice to this day whilst others, although not initiated during his lifetime, are now common practice such as education being the responsibility of the state.

Roger Ascham, John Aylmer, John Fox and Thomas Wilson all received appointments as tutors to children of royalty or nobility. Their pupils included Lady Jane Grey, Elizabeth I and Edward VI, all esteemed intellectually. Richard Croke was a fashionably humanist tutor, educated at Eton followed by King's College, Cambridge where he earned his Bachelor of Arts in 1510. He taught Greek in Leipzig, Germany from 1514 before returning to England in 1519 to become the first official native English professor of Greek at Cambridge, before joining Fitzroy's household and replacing John Palsgrave as Fitzroy's tutor in 1526 through his patron Cardinal Thomas Wolsey. Croke would go on to receive his Doctorate in Divinity in 1524 and would tutor Henry VIII in Greek as it had not formed part of his studies as a child. Croke would be replaced as Fitzroy's tutor, and it is thought this appointment went to George Folbury, who remained in the role until 1531. Folbury graduated from Cambridge in 1514, became a fellow of both Clare and Pembroke Colleges. He was awarded his

Masters in 1517 and was preacher at Cambridge University in 1519, graduating with a Bachelor of Theology in 1524. He is also believed to have studied a Doctorate in Divinity in Montpellier, France. As with most royal and noble children, Fitzroy had more than one tutor, William Saunders was appointed to tutor Fitzroy in music and singing. Saunders was a former servant of Cardinal Thomas Wolsey and had been sent to Sheriff Hutton to instruct Fitzroy.

Although a couple of tutors seem to have spent a period of time in prison courtesy of Henry VIII's quest for an annulment of his marriage to Katharine of Aragon, the worst fate fell upon Richard Fetherston. He was appointed as tutor to Henry and Katharine of Aragon's daughter, Mary. Sadly, Fetherston faced the ultimate punishment when he remained loyal to Mary and his Catholic faith, refusing to sign the Oath of Supremacy, he was hung drawn and quartered in 1540 along with another two individuals whilst three Protestants were burned to death.

Edward's tutors seemed to have fared better than Mary's. Richard Cox was the first to be appointed as official tutor to Edward VI. Cox was a former fellow of King's College, Cambridge. For a number of years, he held the prestigious position of headmaster of Eton School and had also taught at Oxford, was known as a humanist and reformer favoured by Thomas Cranmer who would also likely influence Edward's religious persuasion. Later, in the reign of Edward VI, Cox was appointed Dean of Christ Church, Oxford, and Vice-Chancellor of the University. Cox was not afraid of corporal punishment even when his pupil was of royal blood, there is a possibility he might have physically punished Edward if his royal pupil misbehaved during his lessons. The majority of schoolmasters prior to the Renaissance held with the attitude of the Church that punishment of a child was acceptable as to suffer pain was good for the soul. Many humanist tutors did not agree with this and sought to make education a much more enjoyable experience for children, believing if they enjoyed it, they would likely study to a higher degree and as a result improve themselves. Amongst those who abhorred corporal punishment were Erasmus, Ascham and Elyot.

Cox was allocated an assistant to help him deliver Edward's education and for this role, he chose Sir John Cheke. Although he was initially assistant to Cox, Cheke actually stayed with Edward until he was fourteen. Cheke was a champion of the Renaissance, a successful scholar at Cambridge, he produced a guide for the pronunciation of Greek and was the most famous Greek scholar of his generation. Cheke's education consisted of studying at St John's College, Cambridge before becoming a fellow. In 1540, he was appointed the Regius Professor of Greek at Cambridge where his curriculum included the works of Sophocles, Homer, Herodotus and Euripides and during his lectures used Erasmus' version of Greek pronunciation.[18] His lasting legacy was to be the introduction of the pronunciation of ancient Greek to his pupils one of whom was Roger Ascham, later tutor to Elizabeth. Cheke was a Protestant and fled England on the accession of Mary but converted to Catholicism when he was extradited from the Netherlands. He was of humble birth, supporting the notion that the Tudors promoted academic ability over birth status. He had gone on to become one of the greatest classical scholars of the time and was known to be an encouraging tutor as well as a successful courtier. Cheke was assisted in teaching Edward by Anthony Cooke. Cooke was Cambridge educated and a humanist and is mostly remembered for the exceptional education he provided for his daughters which, like the daughters of Thomas More, was extraordinary for girls at the time. The More girls were also tutored by Nicholas Kratzer, a mathematician and astrologer from Munich. He was recommended to Erasmus and travelled to London in 1517, becoming a friend of Thomas More and tutor to his children before being appointed as astrologer to Henry VIII. Sir Thomas More is renowned for providing an education for his daughters which rivalled that provided for a son and is likely the influence for Cooke's decision to highly educate his daughters.

As we have seen, Edward shared some of his lessons with his sister Elizabeth but there came a point she needed her own tutors. The first was John Picton of which little is known. Next came William Grindal, who came from humble origins. Grindal was a Cambridge scholar, graduated 1541/2 and was admitted as a fellow of St John's College in 1542/3. He was a pupil and later friend of Roger Ascham. In 1544, Grindal was called to the royal household by Cheke to tutor Elizabeth in Greek and he had Ascham's recommendation to approve him for the post. Grindal died in 1548 of the plague and was greatly mourned by Ascham. Edward had a separate music teacher, the appointment awarded to Philip van Wilder who was a favourite musician of Henry VIII. Van Wilder taught Edward to play the lute as well as directed the children of the Privy Chamber in singing. He also taught Henry VIII's daughter, Mary to play lute, regals and virginals and directed the choir at the coronation of Edward VI.

Doubtless, the most remembered of all the royal tutors is Roger Ascham, born c.1515. He enrolled at St John's, Cambridge aged fourteen and received his Bachelor of Arts in 1533 and was elected as a fellow of St John's and reader of Greek before achieving his Masters in 1537. On completion of his Masters, he became a regent master delivering lectures in dialectic, mathematics and Greek. He is known to have deplored corporal punishment, instead, believing a gentle approach would encourage his students to enjoy learning. It is likely Ascham learned this approach from his own tutor Cheke, who he continued to promote as an excellent tutor in his own later writings. Ascham emboldened his students to ask questions, ensuring they understood their subjects as opposed to learning by rote but not actually understanding what they had memorised. He was tutor to Lady Jane Grey and Elizabeth. His most famous work was published posthumously; *The Scholemaster* in 1570 and it proved to be an advance in the theory of education. Ascham supported the views of Vives that children should learn Latin through conversation and supported the theory of commonplace books for pupils to keep notes of sentences, phrases and verses to recall. Ascham wrote:

> There is a waie, touched in the first booke of Cicero De Oratore, which, wiselie brought into scholes, truly taught, and cōstantly vsed, would not onely take wholly away this butcherlie feare in making of latines, but would also, with ease and pleasure, and in short time, as I know by good experience, worke a true choice and placing of words, a right ordering of sentences, an easie vnderstandying of the tonge, a readiness to speake,a facultie to write, a true judgement, both of his owne, and other mens doings, what tonge so euer he doth vse.

And goes on to recommend the study of Horace, Tully, Terence and other classical authors but did not omit religious texts and included study of the Bible in his recommendations for a thorough education.[19]

For his children to study languages, Henry VIII chose Jean Belmaine, a French humanist who was residing in England as a refugee and was appointed to teach French to Edward and Elizabeth in approximately 1545. He had left France to escape the persecution of Protestants. Belmaine translated into French *Lamentacions of a Sinner* which was written by Kathryn Parr and also translated the second Prayer Book of Edward VI. He was known to work his royal charges hard as a rigorous drill master. As a Protestant, it is possible his beliefs influenced the faith of both future monarch's.

There are many men who although they did not tutor royal or noble pupils would have a lasting impact on education. One of these was William Grocyn, he was possibly the first to lecture in Greek at Oxford in the late fifteenth century. Grocyn had become interested in the New Learning prior to the Tudors ascending the throne but his influence continued under their reign. The introduction of the study of Greek at Oxford must have been an exciting opportunity for many scholars who previously might have only known medieval literature. One of Grocyn's most renowned pupils was Thomas More who was studying at Oxford under his patron, Cardinal Morton.[20] Grocyn was a fellow at New College, Oxford between 1465-81 which coincides with the time John Rede, William Horman and John Stanbridge were present, making it possible that all benefitted from Grocyn's teaching and coincidentally became headmasters of established schools and considerable influences on learning.

The most renowned astrologer of the time was John Dee, distinguished not only as the best astrologer, but also the best mathematician and alchemist under the reign of Elizabeth. Dee studied at Cambridge and became a fellow of Trinity College and also studied at Louvain before later becoming astrologer and advisor to Elizabeth I. He tutored Elizabeth and members of her court including Robert Dudley, Philip Sidney and Christopher Hatton and was well known for his expertise in navigation, often being consulted by those making voyages. Dee wished for the creation of a national library which unfortunately was not to happen in his lifetime, so instead, he collected books and manuscripts across the continent until he had the grandest library in England. Sadly, it was vandalised whilst Dee was abroad researching the possibility of conversing with angels and many of his books and manuscripts were stolen or destroyed.

John Foxe is best known for his *Acts and Monuments* (Book of Martyrs) but he was also a scholar and tutor. Foxe attended Oxford achieving his Bachelor of Arts and Masters before lecturing on logic. He resigned from his position due to his religious beliefs contradicting the requirements of the role.[21] He continued to tutor but on a private basis until the accession of Mary I when he left England and worked in Europe before returning under the reign of Elizabeth I. Robert Fayrfax was favoured by Henry VII and was the organist at St Alban's Abbey. He became the first Doctor of Music at Cambridge and continued to serve as royal composer under Henry VIII, even composing music for the Field of Cloth of Gold in 1520.[22]

Whilst not a tutor, the scholar Sir Thomas Elyot was esteemed by his contemporaries and the general public for his work. *The Boke Named the Governor*, published in 1531, was dedicated to Henry VIII and was a moral treatise advising on the education a person should undertake if they wished to obtain a high position within the court. Elyot also argued that the reason for poor standards in education was the low pay received by schoolmasters and due to the low pay, they did not have the status they deserved within society and therefore many who would make excellent schoolmasters would not subject themselves to the position. He also supported the theories of Erasmus and Vives by agreeing that female education was important and published the tract *The Defence of Good Women* in 1540. Elyot believed that educated women would provide a moral education and upbringing for their children. He also wrote *A Castell of Helth,* published in 1541, which was very popular with the general public for its advice on medicine.

It is particularly clear, especially under the early Tudors, that there was a circle of humanist scholars who would become tutors, schoolmasters and influencers of education. All of the royal tutors were engaged with the New Learning and as with all other aspects of Tudor life, everyone sought to imitate the royal court so humanist tutors were sought by all. A number of the tutors and scholars studied together or were taught by one of those mentioned. The majority of the tutors were educated at Winchester College, New College and Magdalen College, highlighting that they were the centres for humanist studies under the Tudors. Henry VIII continued this preferment with the appointment of humanist tutors for his own children. This patronage and appointment provided opportunity for humanists and scholars and enabled humanism to thrive in England which was evident in the next generation.

Chapter Five

Educating the Aristocracy

The aristocracy combined the gentry, nobility, magnates, knights and esquires of the land. For these classes, their educational requirements differed from that of the lower classes in some ways but were the same for the main body of it. Children born to royalty, nobility or the wealthy were often passed into the hands of others such as wet nurses and rockers for care almost immediately. In the early part of the Tudor reign, the education of male nobility was largely concerned with military exercise along with learning courtly etiquette. Military training for boys would commence from a very early age under the guise of toys and games such as pellet guns, crossbows, bow and arrows. For the very young there were toy knights on horseback with wheels they could use to crash into a companion's toy or aim at a target, imitating a cavalry charge they might participate in as an adult. The aristocracy was obliged to provide military assistance to the monarch when required and therefore should be trained in the art of war. Literary education was not a priority and therefore was not considered vital but during the Tudor age literary education amongst the aristocracy including the nobility increased with many receiving instruction in Latin and English grammar. Dependent on their wealth, the nobility didn't often require a full education as they would have people employed for the purposes required such as lawyers and doctors. The gentry were those who mostly advanced their education through specific learning to secure a career. Prior to the Renaissance, Latin was not really a priority for the aristocracy unless they intended to follow a career in the Church or law. The nobility, in particular, had no intention of following these careers and therefore Latin had lost its influence in the education of the nobility from around the twelfth century. The rediscovery of ancient authors revived the study of Latin but even as a single subject this changed throughout the period. Initially, Latin was taught as a language to be spoken so all study revolved around dialogues but as interest increased it became popular to study the Latin the ancient authors had used, a Latin more elegant which appealed to humanists and therefore royalty, nobility and the aristocracy studied it in earnest.

All children irrespective of class were taught courtesy, this would include how to behave in front of others, to bow or curtsey but also many rules that are still common today including not speaking with a full mouth, not interrupting people when they are speaking and keeping elbows off the table. For the aristocratic boys, they would need to learn to carve meat and how to serve the man of the house at his table. For the nobility this was made more difficult due to the large variety of meat served at meals. They would need to know how to dismember each variety and how to serve the meat with its accompanying sauce. Boys and girls would be taught the rules of etiquette such as not taking a drink behind the back of someone important as it was deemed rude. They would need to learn how to wash their hands before and after eating, which today may seem simple but it was a routine in itself. Forks were not a common utensil at the time, children would learn to eat using a knife and sometimes a spoon. Boys and girls of the aristocracy learned to ride from an early age as this was the preferred mode of transport. Although litters were available for females, many chose and preferred to ride. For the boys this formed part of their military training as they would be expected to be able to ride a warhorse if required and had the added benefit of readying them for the joust if they wished to compete and for both boys and girls, enabled them to join the hunt if the opportunity presented itself.

Children of the aristocracy often received a good education but this was dependent on their status, wealth and succession place. For example, two sons might receive the same initial education but further education would differ as the first son would be the heir to the family fortune through the custom of primogeniture, and the second son likely to have to make his own way in the world. This meant to the second son, his success relied on climbing the social ladder and acquiring favour from those of the ranks above him. Unless he wished to take religious orders, he would need to learn to be agreeable within company and make himself useful to his betters. Impressing someone's social betters could lead to the ultimate prize, an appointment at court and possibly royal favour.

With Henry VII and Henry VIII relying more on educated individuals rather than members of the aristocracy to form their council, education became more popular amongst the aristocracy in an attempt to obtain prominent roles. Prior to this, the education of the aristocracy was largely left to other nobility or knightly 'masters' to train boys in warfare with priests or clerks being recruited intermittently for assistance in teaching reading and writing, though this did not cease with the increase in formal literary education. Those of the lower branches of the aristocracy sought a literate education in order to obtain an office such as Sheriff, Justice of the Peace or an administrative role within the royal household whilst those of the nobility sought favour with the monarch and wished to learn in order to further this favour and administer their estates. Some might have even furthered their education with the study of Latin and French, especially those who might have to deal with legal documentation or with overseas correspondence.

Dependent on their wealth, children of the aristocracy might have attended school whilst others would have a tutor employed to teach them at home and therefore had no need to attend school. Another alternative was that they were sent away to the household of a family higher in social rank than their own. Here, they would share a tutor with children from other families and the children of the household, a practice which decreased within the sixteenth century with the increase in the number of tutors and boarding schools. Those fortunate enough to have a private tutor would have studied a similar curriculum to those attending grammar schools but dependent on the skill of their tutor and the intelligence of the pupil, this could advance much further than that provided at a school. Employing tutors within the household was not restricted to boys, many wealthy families employed a tutor for female children or at least allowed them to share the lessons of the male siblings, one such household was that of Sir Thomas More who effectively created a school within his household and provided the very best education for his daughters.

For the extremely fortunate, the household they were sent to could be the royal household where they would share a tutor with the royal children and hopefully secure a friendship with the child which would benefit them in later life. An example of this would be the boys chosen to share the schoolroom of Edward, the boys would share his lessons but also gained the opportunity of forming a friendship such as that between Edward and Barnaby Fitzpatrick who Edward continued to communicate with even whilst Fitzpatrick was abroad. For the majority, early education was received at home where they would learn knowledge of etiquette and the art of making conversation. Girls might learn seemingly feminine skills such as sewing and embroidery and would serve the lady of the house learning how to behave. The extent of these skills would depend on the status of the lady with the ultimate role being Maid of Honour to a grand lady such as a duchess and possibly a princess or the queen. Whilst in another household, girls would learn the skill of household management, this would involve learning how to manage the household accounts, servants and ensuring resources including food and provisions were all in adequate supply. Middle-class aristocracy rarely had the opportunity to progress highly enough to the royal household but they still had the opportunity to attract a beneficial suitor. Religious houses provided much of the education for common children as we shall see in the following chapter but the aristocracy also made use of education provided by religious houses. Priors, abbots and bishops often took in boarders, largely the sons of gentlemen, for a fee and provided the boys with an education in reading and writing as well as courtesy. Thomas More was one such child that received his early education from a religious household.

Even though the custom of sending children away to other households decreased, it remained in practice as a kind of apprenticeship for aristocratic boys. It was not controlled by a guild and was known as the 'knightly order'. This worked as an apprenticeship in that boys would learn and progress through levels; page, squire, bachelor as they gained more experience with the hopeful outcome of a knighthood. Boys were meant to learn the art of chivalry, heraldry, and military skills. The wealthier households would provide a tutor to teach reading, writing and grammar whilst the men-at-arms of the household or those more experienced would teach military skills to those less experienced. These skills would include how to array armour, riding, knowledge of war and rules of the tournament and joust. Boys would be trained in martial sports including archery, wrestling and fighting on foot with various weapons. If they were wealthy or lucky enough to reside in a household with a tilting yard, they would have the opportunity to learn to run at the ring, which would form the training of learning to joust. Running at the ring involved riding on one side of the tilt-yard and aiming to hit a target with a lance. Sometimes the target would be weighted by a sack of sand and if the rider wasn't fast enough could find themselves unhorsed as the sack swung round and hit them. Whilst training, the lance would be fairly light in comparison to that used at a real jousting event. If a boy progressed well, he could eventually joust alongside the king or at least sign up to participate in challenges issued by the monarch for tournaments.

A page in a noble household could expect to start their employment as young as seven years old but would receive an education in grammar, reading and writing, chivalry and heraldry. Courtesy would also be taught which was essential for his progression along with other skills to make him more acceptable at the royal court if he aimed to obtain a place, including carving meat, serving their lord at table, dancing, singing, games such as chess and boys likely learnt to gamble. After a period of seven years as a page, a boy could progress to the role of a squire which was the personal assistant to a knight. As a squire, he would be expected to complete all tasks for his lord at home and accompany his master to the battlefield where he might be fortunate enough to impress and receive his knighthood, although a knighthood was expensive as they were obligated to undertake public services in their locality. For those who could not afford to do this, they could still undertake the training but would instead offer their services to a lord as a bachelor, in exchange for patronage.

The king's household was obviously the most sought after for those wishing to become knights. The Chapel Royal not only had a song master but also a grammar master who would teach the pages and squires in the king's household as well as other children of the nobility. These boys would benefit from the military education provided by the Master of Henchmen, who was responsible for teaching the boys to ride, joust and the correct way of wearing armour. They would also be taught courtly manners and behaviours, including dancing and singing and their table manners would be observed at mealtimes. Their education was not all military and courtesy but also academic. They were taught languages, heraldry and music by the Master of Henchmen whilst a grammar master was tasked with teaching the boys grammar.[1]

Heirs who were too young to succeed to their land or titles upon the death of their father could become a ward of the Crown through the institution of feudal wardship. The Crown could sell wardships which often led to the nobility obtaining the wardship of wealthy heirs and heiresses whose estates they would manage and make use of the income until the child came of age to inherit. This meant their lord was bound to provide them with education and ensure their readiness for their future responsibilities' dependent on their status. Wards would receive the same standard of education and training including martial skills as any natural children of the lord and would share tutors. For royal wards, this often meant they would also be under the supervision of the Master of the Henchmen along with the pages and squires.

Very wealthy girls, such as daughters of the nobility, might be awarded a position at court. These females were brought up with the primary aim to shine at court and attract a beneficial suitor which could bring favour to the family. They were not educated to the same degree as male siblings but were to be able to hold witty conversations and entertain at court events. Dancing and music were vital components of a girl's education as dancing allowed a female to show herself as elegant at entertainments whilst in the company of the most eligible men of the land. A position at court opened possibilities of requesting favours for family and raising the family status through marriage. Twelve years old was the minimum age a girl could debut at court and would be expected to be accomplished in singing and dancing. Fathers had the option of settling their daughters at a nunnery, this was often an option where there were many daughters and it would prove extremely expensive to provide dowries for each daughter. Sending a daughter to a nunnery was a cheaper option than the cost of finding a husband and marrying them off. Girls could also make this choice themselves of course but during this time it was the father that retained the ultimate decision. Nunneries for wealthy girls gave the prospect of education, gaining responsibility and gaining a career within the nunnery and girls could progress to the role of abbess. Some nunneries also provided an education, without obligation of the daughter becoming a nun. Those that offered teaching often did so to supplement the income of the nunnery and would accept boys and girls although it is doubtful the education was of the same high quality as that a monastery or alternative school could provide. Daughters of the aristocracy often had the time and ability to work on translating texts and if they were under the instruction of tutors were often set tasks on translating works of a moral or biblical nature. The daughters of Anthony Cooke, tutor to Edward, were also renowned for translating works.

Males of the nobility would learn posturing from tutors, dance masters or through observation at court and aimed to distinguish themselves from the lower classes by swaggering, causing their swords and daggers to jingle as they walked, the resulting sound indicating their social status. For those seeking a position in the royal household or that of a nobleman, grammar school could be the first stepping stone. The aim of the grammar school was to provide a more in-depth education to those of the wealthier class but many did accept those of the lower classes. It was largely the sons of the gentry who attended grammar schools under the Tudors and they mostly began to attend between the ages of nine and twelve although there are records that some enrolled as early as seven years old. These exceptions would not have attended a petty school but might have received private tuition from an early age to ensure they were capable of meeting the expectations for entry to a grammar school. Erasmus and other humanists believed education should certainly start younger than nine.

Those who attended grammar school would receive a classical education, learning to read, understand, speak and write Latin, which was the language used by scholars and the Church. Dependent on the school, Greek was also an option especially towards the end of the period. The routine at grammar schools was often strict, at Eton School, the boys had to wake up before 5.00 am and recite prayers whilst making their beds before beginning lessons at 6.00 am.[2] The morning lessons commonly lasted until 11.00 am, then resumed in the afternoon from 1.00 pm to 6.00 pm. In the winter, the school day would be shortened by around two hours. Unlike today there were few holidays with the only regular holidays being at Christmas, Easter and Whitsun and there was certainly no long summer break. The children would learn to read, if they hadn't done so already at an elementary level, using a hornbook which was a piece of wood with the alphabet or reading exercises printed on that was covered with a layer of horn for protection. At grammar school, it is probable most had already learnt the alphabet and basic prayers so the hornbook would be used for more advanced texts. Children of the aristocracy would likely own their own hornbook to assist them in their learning. Writing was not guaranteed to be taught at all grammar schools and was taught separately from reading. Most city and large town grammar schools likely did teach writing. For those fortunate to have a schoolmaster capable of teaching writing they would be taught to write in English and Latin and some grammar schools even expected basic writing skills as a prerequisite for enrolling. For others, they would have to learn to write through the teachings of a separate writing master, incurring a further fee or through travelling scriveners who offered writing lessons. For boys of the aristocracy, their interest in grammar was to assist them in administrative duties as an adult rather than wishing to understand linguistic aspects of the language. The focus for these boys was the study of dictamen, the art of composing letters. Some grammar schools would employ specialist schoolmasters to teach these skills to those that wished to further their study past the basic standard taught to all. This skill would be beneficial in enabling the boys to learn to draft a variety of letters and was a valuable experience to those who would later enrol at one of the Inns of Court.[3]

The pupils would have to listen to their tutor recite texts which they would have to learn by rote, as children of wealthy families they likely had notebooks which were known as commonplace books to write memorable passages or phrases in to help them memorise the work. Most grammar schools based their curriculum on the *trivium* – grammar, logic and rhetoric. This might appear to be a very basic curriculum but it actually covered a multitude of topics including English and Latin grammar, the composition of verse and prose, history and geography as well as the vital subject of religion. One of the most common teaching methods for Latin and Greek was to memorize the text then repeat it to the tutor and translate the text from Latin or Greek into English and then back again, known as double translation. The pupils would continue to do this until they could speak and write eloquently in the language being studied. Double translation was used in schools and by private tutors including Roger Ascham and John Cheke.

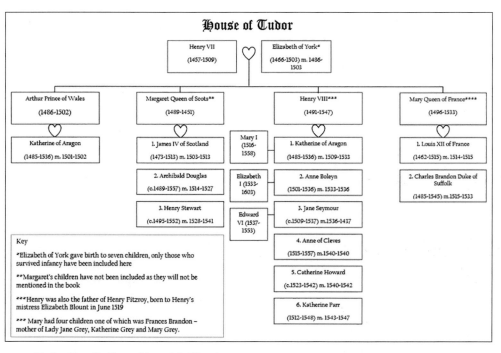

House of Tudor

Henry VII (1457-1509)	♡	Elizabeth of York* (1466-1503) m. 1486-1503

Arthur Prince of Wales (1486-1502)	Margaret Queen of Scots** (1489-1451)	Henry VIII*** (1491-1547)	Mary Queen of France**** (1496-1533)

Arthur Prince of Wales ♡
Katherine of Aragon (1485-1536) m. 1501-1502

Margaret Queen of Scots ♡
1. James IV of Scotland (1473-1513) m. 1503-1513
2. Archibald Douglas (c.1489-1557) m. 1514-1527
3. Henry Stewart (c.1495-1552) m. 1528-1541

Henry VIII ♡
Mary I (1516-1558)
Elizabeth I (1533-1603)
Edward VI (1537-1553)

1. Katherine of Aragon (1485-1536) m. 1509-1533
2. Anne Boleyn (1501-1536) m. 1533-1536
3. Jane Seymour (c.1509-1537) m.1536-1437
4. Anne of Cleves (1515-1557) m.1540-1540
5. Catherine Howard (c.1523-1542) m. 1540-1542
6. Katherine Parr (1512-1548) m. 1543-1547

Mary Queen of France ♡
1. Louis XII of France (1462-1515) m. 1514-1515
2. Charles Brandon Duke of Suffolk (1485-1545) m.1515-1533

Key

*Elizabeth of York gave birth to seven children, only those who survived infancy have been included here

**Margaret's children have not been included as they will not be mentioned in the book

***Henry was also the father of Henry Fitzroy, born to Henry's mistress Elizabeth Blount in June 1519

*** Mary had four children one of which was Frances Brandon – mother of Lady Jane Grey, Katherine Grey and Mary Grey.

Tudor Family Tree. (Amy McElroy)

KING HENRY THE EIGHTH.

Dean, T. A., printmaker. Henry VIII, King of England, 1491-1547, depicted, engraved by T. A. Dean of an original by Hans Holbein. 19th century. (Call# ART File H521 no.6. Used by permission of the Folger Shakespeare Library under a Creative Commons Attribution-ShareAlike 4.0 International License)

Arthur, Prince of Wales, Stained Glass window at St Laurence' Church, Ludlow. (Amy McElroy)

Edward, Prince of Wales, Stained Glass window at St Laurence's Church, Ludlow. (Amy McElroy)

Above: King Henry VIII and his three children; Will Summers, the King's jester is in the background. Engraving by F. Bartolozzi after H. Holbein the Younger, ca. 1790. (Wellcome Collection. Attribution 4.0 International [CC BY 4.0])

Left: Huys, Frans, Magnus ille Erasmus Roterodamus..., (Call# ART Vol. a11 no.105. Used by permission of the Folger Shakespeare Library under a Creative Commons Attribution-ShareAlike 4.0 International License)

Portrait of John Colet. (Wellcome Collection. Attribution 4.0 International [CC BY 4.0])

Sir Thomas More. Etching by J. Houbraken after H. Holbein. (Wellcome Collection. Public Domain Mark)

Robert Boissard, Portret van Juan Luis Vives, Joannes Ludovicus Vives philosophus, 1597-1599. (Rijksmuseum, Amsterdam)

A schoolroom; illustrating Biblical proverbs on the necessity of the discipline of children. Engraving by H. Goltzius. (Wellcome Collection. Attribution 4.0 International [CC BY 4.0])

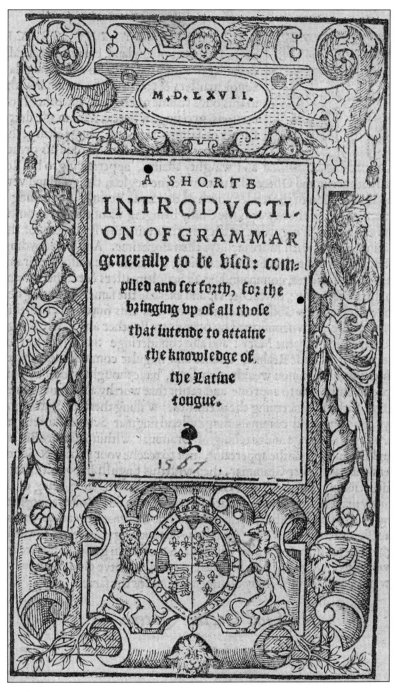

M.D.LXVII.

A SHORTE
INTRODVCTI-
ON OF GRAMMAR
generally to be vsed: compiled and set forth, for the
bringing vp of all those
that intende to attaine
the knowledge of,
the Latine
tongue.

1567

Lily, William, 1468?-1522, A shorte introduction of grammar generally
to be vsed: compiled and set forth, for the bringing vp of all those that
intende to attaine the knowledge of the Latine tongue, (1567). (Call# STC
15614.2. Used by permission of the Folger Shakespeare Library under a
Creative Commons Attribution-ShareAlike 4.0 International License)

Buste van Marcus Tullius Cicero, Hans Witdoeck, after Peter Paul Rubens, after anonymous, 1638. (Rijksmuseum, Amsterdam. Public Domain)

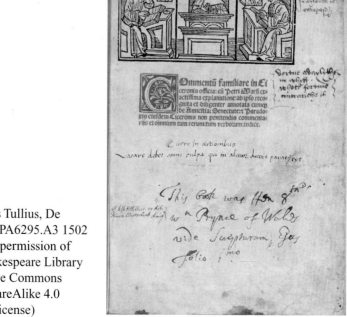

Cicero, Marcus Tullius, De Officia. (Call# PA6295.A3 1502 Cage. Used by permission of the Folger Shakespeare Library under a Creative Commons Attribution-ShareAlike 4.0 International License)

Virgilius, Cicero en Seneca bij Grammatica met leerlingen, Jacobus Harrewijn, 1694. (Rijksmuseum, Amsterdam, Gift of G.J. Boekenoogen, Leiden)

Julius Caesar te paard, Adriaen Collaert, after Jan van der Straet, 1587 – 1589.
(Rijksmuseum, Amsterdam. Public Domain)

OUR father whiche art in
heauen, halowed be thy name.
Thy kyngdome come.
Thy will bee dooen in pearth,
as it is in heauen.
Geue vs this dai our daily bꝛeade
And foꝛgeue vs our trefpaces,
as we foꝛgeue them that trefpace
againſt vs.
And let vs not bee led into temptacion.
But deliuer vs from euill. Amen.

The falutacion of the angell to the bleſſed virgin Mari.

HAile Mari full of grace, the Loꝛde is with thee:
Bleſſed art thou among women, and bleſſed is
the fruict e of thy wombe. Amen.

¶ *The Crede, oꝛ.rii. articles of the Chꝛiſten faith.*

Beleue in GOD the father almightie,
maker of heauen and pearth.
And in Jeſu Chꝛiſt his only ſone our loꝛd
Whiche was conceiued by the holy
goſt, boꝛne of the virgin Mari.
Suffered vnder Ponce Pilate, was crucified, dead
buried, and defcended into hell.
And the thirde daie, he rofe again from death.
He afcended into heauen, and fitteth on the right
hande of God the father almightie.
From thence he ſhall come to iudge the quicke, and
the dead.

Jbeliug

Beleue in the holy goſt. The holy catholike
church. The Communion of faintes the foꝛ:
geueneſſe of finnes. The refurreccion of the
body. And the life euerlaſtyng.

The ten commaundementes of almightie God.

Thou ſhalt haue none other godes but me
Thou ſhalt not haue any graue Image
noꝛ any likeneſſe of any thyng, that is in
heauen aboue, oꝛ in the pearth beneth, oꝛ
in the water vnder the pearth, to thintent
to dooe any godly honour oꝛ woꝛſhip vnto them.
Thou ſhalt not take þ name of thy loꝛd God in vain.
Remembꝛe that thou kepe holy the Sabboth daie.
Honour thy father and thy mother.
Thou ſhalt dooe no murdꝛe.
Thou ſhalt not commit adultry.
Thou ſhalt not ſteale.
Thou ſhalt not beare falfe witnes againſt thy neigh:
boure.
Thou ſhalt not vniuſtly defire thy neighbours houfe
noꝛ thy neighbours wife, noꝛ his feruaunt, noꝛ his
mayde, noꝛ his Oxe, noꝛ his Aſſe, noꝛ any thyng that is
thy neighbours.

LOꝛde, into thy handes J commende my fpirite:
Thou haſt redemed me, loꝛde God of trueth.

¶ *Grace before diner.*

The iyes of all thynges truſte in the, O loꝛde,
Thou geueſt them meate in due feafõ. Thou
dooeſt open thy hande, and filleſt with thy
bleſſyng euery liuyng thyng. Good loꝛde
bleſſe

C.iii.

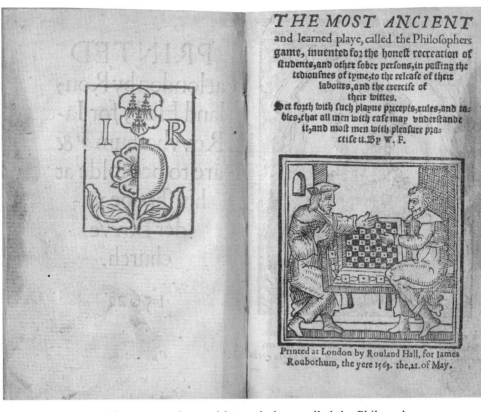

Lever, Ralph, The most ancient and learned playe, called the Philosophers game, inuented for the honest recreation of students, and other sober persons, in passing the tediousnes of tyme, to the release of their labours, and the exercise of their wittes, 1563. (Call# STC 15542 Bd.w. STC 6214 Copy 1. Used by permission of the Folger Shakespeare Library under a Creative Commons Attribution-ShareAlike 4.0 International License)

Shakespearian representation before Queen Elizabeth [graphic]. (Call# ART File S527.4 no.27 (size L). Used by permission of the Folger Shakespeare Library under a Creative Commons Attribution-ShareAlike 4.0 International License)

Renaissance Drawing, woman with lute. (Wikimedia Commons, Creative Commons Attribution-Share Alike 4.0 International)

Fig. 187 —The Dance called "La Gaillarde."—Fac-simile of Wood Engravings from the "Orchésographie" of Thoinot Arbeau (Jehan Tabourot): 4to (Langres, 1588).

Woodcut of people dancing a galliard, Paul Lacroix, Manners, Custom and Dress During the Middle Ages and During the Renaissance Period. (Wikimedia Commons, Public domain)

Joust from a 1550 book of jousts and tournaments. (Wikimedia Commons, Public Domain)

Hendrick Goltzius, Koningen Hendrik VIII en Edward VI, koninginnen Mary en Elizabeth, Koningen en koninginnen van Engeland (series title), 1584. (Rijksmuseum, Amsterdam)

Translating the works of the classics such as Aristotle, Demosthenes and Plato would ensure the boys remembered the theories presented so they could then discuss these in company, showing their intellectual abilities. Erasmus argued that imitation was the best form of education 'nature has equipped children with a unique urge to imitate whatever they hear or see; they do this with great enthusiasm, as though they were monkeys, and are overjoyed if they think they have been successful' and goes on to say that through imitation it is possible to instil intelligent literature just as easily as it is for children to learn jokes and songs. 'What is to hinder them from learning delightful tales, witty aphorisms, memorable incidents from history, or intelligent fables with no greater effort than that with which they pick up and absorb stupid, often vulgar ballads, ridiculous old wives' tales, and all sorts of tedious womanish gossip?'[4] When reading the classics, pupils were encouraged to place themselves in the same situation, and ask how would they act? This was meant to instil virtue and morality and provide an exemplum of behaviours to follow when they reached adulthood.

A basic humanist curriculum would consist of the Latin works of Cicero, Livy and Pliny and Greek works of Euripides, Plutarch and Thucydides amongst others. These works cover oratory, grammar and history. Boys could obviously expand on this curriculum if they were inclined to do so. If they were capable, they could begin the *quadrivium* – arithmetic, geometry, music and astronomy which might cover the philosophy of Aristotle and Thomas Aquinas. This advanced stage would not be as in-depth as the quadrivium provided at the universities. Boys at grammar school were generally not taught French, this was a language learned by the nobility and royalty or those who would be required to learn Law French if they attended the Inns of Court after grammar school.

Historical events such as the tales of Agincourt would be learned as they provided boys with knowledge on history but also military knowledge and strategy. A further work popular with the aristocracy was a text which was initially intended for the Roman army, *Epitoma Rei Militaris* written by Vegetius in the fourth century. It was published in English in the fifteenth century and became the standard book for military training and of course, provided a historical account of the training of the Romans. The work recommended a number of physical sports to form part of a boy's education including weights, jousting and riding.

Children today will spend part of their week doing Physical Education and it was no different in the sixteenth century although the subject differed. Boys would be taught archery and those of means taught hawking and to hunt. Music also formed part of the curriculum with children being taught to play instruments that varied according to the school and were often taught to sing. For the aristocracy, learning to play instruments, sing and dance also meant they might be noticed at court and hopefully find favour and might even find themselves entertaining the monarch if they performed well enough. *The Boke Called the Governour* written by Sir Thomas Elyot in 1531 encouraged noblemen to learn to play instruments stating it was an important skill for a courtier but advised men to play in private as to not appear arrogant. All those at the royal court might be expected to provide entertainment at some point, in the form of playing an instrument, singing or dancing and therefore it was important that all were accomplished regardless of gender.

Sir Thomas More, born 1478, is probably the most celebrated English scholar of the time. He was the son of Sir John More, a lawyer and judge. He began his formal education at the age of approximately seven years old. His first school, St Anthony's in London, was an almonry school, attached to an institution providing care for the elderly. The priests used their knowledge of Latin to provide an education to the sons of wealthy merchants and the gentry. Thomas More's curriculum was based on the *trivium,* the same used in neighbouring schools, although the exact lesson details are unknown. At approximately twelve years old, he left St Anthony's school and joined the household of Cardinal

Morton, Archbishop of Canterbury. Here, Thomas More was to learn etiquette and how to behave in such a household. As with all boys who were sent to another household, he would have learnt how to serve at the table including the carving of meat and looking after guests, but he would also travel with the archbishop as he moved between his residencies, ensuring his belongings were secure and needs met. The experience introduced Thomas More to society and earned him a wealthy patron, who secured a placement for him at Oxford University when he was fourteen years old.

On completion of grammar school, aged approximately fourteen, some boys would attend one of the university colleges at Oxford or Cambridge where their studies would include grammar, logic, philosophy and rhetoric. The three philosophies of Aristotle; *Nichomachean Ethics, Eudemian Ethics* and the *Magna moralia* were still the principal sources at the beginning of the period. Attending university was not necessarily to achieve a degree, many attended in order to expand their education but not to necessarily earn a degree and sought simply to attend one of the university colleges as a finishing school before possibly ending their formal education or moving on to one of the Inns of Court. Others might travel abroad to finish their education, attending lectures at European universities or where opportunity enabled, visiting foreign royal courts to polish their courtly etiquette and languages as well as create a social network.

Although the universities are noted here as venues of education for the aristocracy, at the beginning of the Tudor age they were predominantly attended by men of the Church both of common and aristocratic status, but the purposes of the colleges were changing as many sought an education for career advancement and toward the end of the Tudor age the majority of pupils were children of the gentry. The very wealthy had additional privileges at university, they could pay additional fees to sit and eat with the fellows of the college and could even bring their servants and own tutors with them. The arts faculty offered the most basic course, which at Oxford lasted four years and consisted of dialectic, grammar and logic, which on completion would result in a Bachelor of Arts. Early in the period, logic was losing some of its value as was scholasticism as the interest in humanism grew and spread. Although logic wasn't replaced entirely, the colleges focused more on rhetoric and literary grammar as opposed to its linguistic properties. At this level, the study of grammar consisted of the origins and meaning of words and texts. A further three years of study, mostly of philosophy plus two years teaching at the school, was required to obtain a Master of Arts. Studies in canon or civil law, medicine or theology were known as the higher faculties and were effectively post-graduate and could not be studied without first completing the Bachelor of Arts, with the exception of law which could be studied without a Bachelor of Arts but years would be added to the course duration meaning it would not save any time by not completing the Bachelor of Arts prior to beginning the study of law. The study of grammar could continue to a higher level. These men would become known as grammarians and would undertake the study of Latin and Greek texts in their original form on a variety of subjects from the sacred texts to history and philosophy.

By the mid-sixteenth century, pupils could also study a degree and a doctorate in Music but it was not regarded as highly as the other subjects and there were few graduates. For the higher faculties, canon and civil law were the most popular as they provided graduates with the most opportunities. Men of the Church could progress through the church the more they studied, receiving higher beneficiaries whilst those studying civil law could teach in the profession and if they wished, could continue on to the Inns of Chancery or Inns of Court. For anyone wishing to become a doctor of canon law, they would be required to undertake three years civil law study, followed by teaching canon law for five years. This might seem like a long route to a doctorate but the longest was by far the course to a Doctorate in Divinity which could last seventeen years as theology was seen as the highest faculty. Theology was most common amongst monks and friars, and even after the Reformation members of the clergy continued to study to Masters level, providing England with a body of highly educated clergy.

Thomas More and other students studied a curriculum of the *quadrivium* – astronomy, geometry, music and arithmetic. Those who completed this curriculum would be awarded a Bachelor of Arts, and could continue at the university studying further subjects if they wished. Thomas More was privileged to be able to attend lectures in Greek, newly introduced to Oxford by William Grocyn. As a keen theologian, he was disappointed he could not continue with his studies at the university, as his father was determined he should study common law. It was not unusual for boys to spend some time at university in between grammar school and the path to a specific career.

At Cardinal College, Oxford, the professors of humanities were tasked with delivering two lectures per day. Scholars could attend a lecture on rhetoric in the morning and other topics including Greek in the afternoon. Some students were lucky enough to hear lectures by the king's own astronomer, Nicholas Kratzer, who lectured in geography and astronomy at Oxford, following a request from Henry VIII. Throughout the period the colleges began to appoint lecturers for different levels of students showing consideration was being given to pupil's depending on their time at the college.

There were a number of rules at the university colleges including when and where games could be played, the keeping of animals and dancing in the hall was prohibited. If found to have broken the rules, pupils could be fined or barred from entering the common areas for a period of time. The pupils were expected to always speak Latin to assist in their fluency. Pupils at the university colleges were assigned to a tutor who would have the responsibility of around six pupils. The tutor would not only be responsible for their learning but also provide moral instruction and would retain the allowances of the wealthy pupils, paying their bills on their behalf and ensuring they completed all required tasks of their studies.

The four Inns of Court; Gray's Inn, Inner Temple, Middle Temple and Lincoln's Inn provided an education in common law as they sought to educate and train their own recruits, whilst the universities retained the teaching of canon and civil law. The Inns of Court wished to instil a consistent approach to law and ensure its recruits all met the same standards and held the professional ideals deemed required of the profession. Common law proceedings were conducted in English and French whilst civil and canon law were strictly conducted in Latin. The Inns developed through a guild with the aim of setting standards for entry into the legal profession but progressed into the Inns of Court and the lesser Inns of Chancery which acted as preparation for those entering the Inns of Court. These were not restricted to those wishing to become lawyers and the Tudor period saw an increase in the number of students spending time at the inns to learn enough to help them administer their lands or enable them to be appointed as a magistrate, this was particularly so for gentry and lesser nobles who might not have the resources to retain a lawyer. Early in the Tudor period, Oxford was the centre of education for those wishing to study to help them with their ability to manage business ventures including accounting skills and dictamen but students began to choose the Inns of Court for education in the composition of deeds, charters and other legal documents, resulting in the study of dictamen decreasing at Oxford.

The training to qualify in law was a lengthy procedure and expensive, resulting in the majority of pupils being from the aristocracy, mostly the gentry. Most who wished to qualify would first spend a year or two at the Inns of Chancery where they would be taught the skill of drafting writs. For some this might suffice and therefore they might not need to move on to one of the Inns of Court. Those who did move on to one of the four Inns of Court would be admitted as an 'inner barrister'. Those enrolling at the Inns were expected to already be proficient in Latin and have knowledge of Law French which the majority would have undertaken at either grammar school, or with private tutors and likely developed by spending a period of time at Oxford or Cambridge, where they also might have studied a little canon or civil law as an additional benefit to the study of common law.[5] Once admitted they would begin a very technical curriculum of plea rolls, readings, case studies and could attend hearings at Westminster Hall. Law students today will be familiar with moots or mock trials, and for those studying at the Inns, it was no different but far more frequent as this is how their abilities were assessed. After attending lectures or a reading by one of the lawyers, students would debate the points raised and attempt to apply the principles of law to their argument whilst their tutor would observe and assess them. After a period of seven years, the pupil would be eligible as an 'utter barrister'.

Thomas More left Oxford aged sixteen and enrolled at New Inn, one of the Inns of Chancery. His initial studies gave him the basic learning on the foundations of law and the judicial system. After this, he moved to Lincoln's Inn, enrolling on 12 February 1496, where he studied the law in depth and became familiar with the more controversial aspects of civil law and by his early twenties had gained the knowledge and experience to set up his own practice.[6] He would go on to be an instrumental part of Henry VIII's council, knighted and made Lord Chancellor. The records of the Inns show a large number of sons of aristocracy enrolling and also give an indication of the rules within the Inns. A number of students were fined for gambling within the common hall of the Inn amongst other misdemeanours such as hunting coneys on the lands of the Inn.[7]

For those wishing to study the higher faculty of medicine, the student first had to complete a Bachelor of Arts. On completing their Bachelor of Arts, students had to study for a further four years in medicine to earn their medical degree. If wishing to progress even further, they could study for another two years to become a doctor and then teach for two years to obtain a Master's degree. The majority of medical students would learn a Latin poem that had originally been written in the eleventh century at Salerno University which described the benefits of certain foods and the negative effects of other stimuli but the renaissance led to hundreds of ancient Greek texts being rediscovered which would improve the study of medicine including the work of Galen, a Greek physician who moved to Rome in 163 AD as the physician of Emperor Marcus Aurelius. Despite this, medical training was very academic and based on the literature rather than any practical exercises. The most successful doctors often spent a period abroad learning as English medical training was not at such a high standard until the founding of the Royal College of Physicians, by royal charter in 1518, to improve and regulate the curriculum. Even abroad the training was more theoretical and little practical training was given with dissections often being a spectator learning process until 1540 when Henry VIII granted the Royal College of Surgeons four bodies per year from the gallows at Tyburn. The Tudors believed everything was based on the four humours dry, moist, hot and cold, representing the four elements or blood, phlegm, yellow bile and black bile, dependent on if they studied Aristotle or Hippocrates. They thought if a person was ill there was an imbalance in the humours that needed to be rebalanced. Those studying medicine spent time learning astrology as they believed the stars were linked to the humours and therefore horoscopes were used to consider a person's health, although only the wealthy could afford this. Astronomy was a common subject under the Tudors, especially Henry VII. Astrologers would draw up charts of the monarchs and their families to predict their futures such as life expectancy and successes they would accomplish. The Tudors were fairly superstitious and placed faith in these predictions but it could also be dangerous to predict such things especially if predictions were wrong. Due to its popularity, the aristocracy would study it and discuss theories and study the skies.

Further improvements to the study of medicine were made in 1582 when public lectures on surgery began to be given by the London College of Physicians. These lectures would also have benefitted those wishing to become a Barber-Surgeon. These men took on the physical tasks that doctors appear not to have done. Armies often had barber-surgeons in their company for the treatment of soldiers. The Company of Barber-Surgeons, formed in 1540, was much more practical in its delivery of education, as expected, than that of the doctors but did have weekly lectures for its apprentices. It was not until near the end of the Tudor period that exams were introduced for the testing of apprentices at the end of their term which was usually seven years. Doctors and surgeons were not the only members of the medical profession. Apothecaries were more affordable than doctors and could provide remedies and advice. Lastly, there were midwives, a profession that was open to women but there was no academic training and it was the result of on-the-job learning and experience and was usually the role of lower-class women although there were no rules prohibiting classes from undertaking it. Gentlewomen would often treat locals with herbal remedies and salves that they had created in their still rooms or kitchens. This learning was often done through childhood by imitating their mother or the lady of the house to which they were sent but books became popular on the subject during the period. The presence of a woman with this knowledge could provide immense benefit to those unable to afford the services of an apothecary or the cost of ingredients to make remedies and salves themselves. Most girls would learn at least a little about herbal remedies. Some boys would also take an interest and would learn to make their own tinctures and pastilles.

Those wishing to study medicine were not the only ones to travel abroad, sons of the nobility were often sent on a tour of Europe in an effort to practice language skills, attend lectures and improve their courtly behaviours. For those interested in warfare, this gave them the opportunity to learn about other countries tactics, fortifications and gunnery whilst others could take advantage of the expanse of Renaissance art and literature available abroad. The young men who took these tours were accompanied by their tutor and servants and would travel to cities of renowned intellect and culture. One such man was William Blount, who whilst abroad, would meet Erasmus and later become a companion to Henry VIII.

The Renaissance affected some subjects more than others, neither canon, civil nor common law were affected as most legal literature was based on the old Roman Empire texts which were written in Latin and therefore were already in use. There were few ancient Greek writings based on law. Unfortunately for Thomas More, he received his education as humanist interests were spreading which meant he did not receive the full benefit of a humanist education but he continued to study even after he was qualified as a lawyer. Humanism introduced Greek and Hebrew to the universities, encouraging scholars to study the scriptures in their original form. Thomas More would ensure all of his children received a humanist education including his daughters by setting up an informal school within his household. His daughters were females of exceptional education for the time, they became a model of female education. All of Thomas More's daughters are known to have been intelligent, studying Latin, Greek philosophy, music, astronomy and mathematics, something that was rare for the times. The girls were taught to write in the fashionable italic hand that become so popular with the Renaissance rather than the traditional cursive style which their father would have been taught. In particular, Margaret More-Roper, his eldest daughter, is well known to have been highly educated and she is known to have undertaken a translation of Erasmus' *Devout Treatise upon the Pater Noster*. Margaret was also able to identify mistakes in the Latin writings of Erasmus and the daughters were praised by Juan Luis Vives in his eulogy to *The Education of a Christian Woman*.[8] When considering the education of his son Fitzroy, Henry VIII discussed the learning of Greek with Thomas More. Henry VIII had not learnt Greek himself and the daughters of Thomas More were brought to court to display their skill in the language to the admiration of those present and to show Henry VIII the benefits of studying the language.[9]

The Education of a Christian Woman provided a practical guide for the education of females including appropriate reading material. Reading works of romance was forbidden and girls were encouraged to read only works that pertain to religion, virtue and morality. Vives recommended the Bible and the classical writings of Cicero, Plato, Seneca, Boethius and Tertullian as appropriate for aristocratic girls along with Thomas More's *Utopia* and Erasmus' *Education of a Christian Prince* for those of the nobility.[10] The recommended learning provided by Vives didn't alter much between boys and girls with the exception of recommended oratorical works for boys who were required to be competent in public speaking and the ability to debate whereas girls were not expected to do so and were to remain humble. Another exceptional female was Lady Jane Grey, praised by Ascham for her intellect. Lady Jane studied Spanish, French, Italian, Greek and Latin as a child before progressing to Arabic, Hebrew and Chaldee (the language of the ancient Chaldeans), a very impressive feat for anyone to accomplish but especially a female at the time.[11]

Boys and girls of the aristocracy often undertook the method of double translation whereby they would translate a passage, often Latin, into English and then later translate it back into the original language. This method was also used in the royal household by tutors including Roger Ascham and John Cheke. Many of the aristocracy would continue this exercise into adulthood, translating works as a pastime and to maintain their fluency in languages as well as impress those who would read the finished result. The education of aristocratic boys had three aspects; military, arts and literary. To become an accomplished courtier, they would ideally need to master all three but for the lower classes, none of these were essential but no less desirable. For girls, household management was the principal aim and remained so regardless of class, although as imagined the difference in the size of the household could be vast.

Chapter Six

Educating the Common People

Children from lower social classes such as the children of husbandmen, craftsmen and labourers, were very lucky to have the opportunity to attend school. Unless they had the opportunity to be sent by a wealthy patron, they were likely to only ever attend a petty school followed by a grammar school in some circumstances if a place could be obtained free of charge. The majority of children from lower classes did not learn to read and write as it was assumed there was no benefit to this. Most did not need to be literate in their work and the opportunities requiring literacy were too far above on the social ladder than most could hope of reaching. For the majority of the children of the lower classes, their education came in the form of learning transferable skills which would enable them to find employment when they grew up. Those of the middle class might receive a formal education but this depended largely on the wealth of the family and the time they could commit to their education. It should be noted that whilst wealthy individuals such as merchants or lawyers did not have titles their wealth opened up possibilities of climbing the social ladder especially as the Tudors were keen to employ men of high intellect. If they were successful in their ambitions, they might well find themselves with a title. For those with wealth, their children's education was likely to be more similar to that of the aristocracy than the poorer children.

Children of the lower classes were taught courtesy. Just like those of the aristocracy, they would be taught how to greet people of rank by doffing their cap and the usual manners taught to all. Although they would be taught to bow and curtsey, unlike the aristocracy they were not expected to be able to perform the perfect pose unless it was thought they would be meeting those it would be required for.

This would typically be the wealthier families of the common people who might come into contact with the aristocracy and nobility. The lower classes would likely not need the complex rules of table manners the royal and aristocratic children had to learn as they would likely not have to carve many varieties of meat at a table, or adhere to the rules of the court mealtime rituals. Children of wealthier common families would have learned to ride from an early age, starting with a pony before progressing to a horse. Children of yeomen and husbandmen, although many were not wealthy, also likely leant to ride as their father would use one horse or more for farm work, whilst those of labourer's might not have the opportunity to learn to ride.

If a child was going to attend school, their first would be a dame school which taught children of both sexes up to the age of seven. The dame schools were not strictly academic and taught other skills such as sewing and spinning, a skill a young girl could practice at home. After dame school came petty schools which provided free education for children from the age of seven to approximately fourteen although those who would be attending a grammar school would usually leave their petty school between the ages of nine and twelve. The aim of the petty school was to provide a sound basis in religion and a foundation in Christian doctrine along with an elementary level of grammar in those schools with the capability to provide it. The elementary level of grammar taught to children attending petty schools involved learning the basics in pronunciation before attempting the construction of sentences as well as learning to spell and read using the hornbook and primer which consisted of prayers and psalms. At the end of the fifteenth century, most children, especially those of the lower classes could not afford parchment or paper and therefore the hornbook was still in use. The hornbook was a rectangular wooden board on which paper with writing on was attached and then covered with a transparent sheet of horn for protection. Some had string attached so it could be hung from the child's waist or around their neck. Unlike the children of the aristocracy, it is unlikely the children of the lower classes owned their own hornbook unless it had been passed down the generations.

Song school was another option, aptly named as they were intended to teach boys to sing to become part of the church or monastery choir. Those linked to the monasteries, particularly the Benedictine houses, were largely maintained through charitable donations and bequests left in wills by wealthy benefactors. Song schools were usually attached to the local church or monastery and if the monks had the skill, they would also teach the boys to read and write in Latin and sometimes English. If not, a master might be hired to teach the boys, dependent on the wealth of the monastery. The boys at song school would be taught to sing Latin hymns. Some song schools would teach their pupils to read Latin so the boys could read the hymns themselves whilst others didn't actually understand what they were singing and instead learnt the words by memory. Although this was unlikely to happen in small towns or villages, many aristocrats sought the best singers to become part of their own household or choir, the most prevalent being the Chapel Royal so there was always a small opportunity that a poor child could end up singing for a prominent family or the monarch. For those who managed to get a placement within the royal or a noble household, they would likely receive a much better education than they ever thought likely. The boys of the Chapel Royal were placed under the supervision of the Master of the Children, responsible for their welfare and education. The boys would continue with their musical education but would also receive teaching in reading writing and possibly grammar. The boys would often live with the master making it cost-effective for their parents as well as being an honour to have a child in the royal choir. The boys who obtained places in wealthy households might also have the opportunity to take part in masques and pageants for their patron. The boys of the Chapel Royal certainly appeared in pageants and other entertainments at the royal court.

Some song schools had a reading school that would make use of the psalter; a book containing the psalms along with other devotions and liturgy of the saints, to teach reading in Latin. Pupils who wished to study grammar might be able to do so at some of the reading schools on the provision of an additional fee.[1] Almonry schools were supervised by the almoner and often boys could board at these schools which might also offer tutoring in grammar and Latin, like the song schools they were initially created to provide for the needs of the monasteries and church, and were maintained through charity and payment of fees from those who could afford them. The education provided was much the same as that provided by the schools maintained by secular churches. The number of chantries increased prior to the Tudor period as wealth increased and more individuals wished to found a chantry for Masses to be said for their soul. The increase in the number of chantries resulted in an increased number of chantry schools. These schools were able to provide religious instruction along with the basics in grammar and English reading, sometimes writing, but with the dissolution of the monasteries, the chantries were destroyed along with the majority of these elementary schools, unless they were saved by a wealthy patron or the community. After attending one of the schools provided by the religious houses some of the pupils would have chosen to remain within the religious house and become monks but they were not obliged to do so.

The education of a girl differed; her fate ultimately depended on whether her family required her to stay at home to provide labour. If she could be spared a girl might attend a dame or petty school but she would be very unlikely to receive any further education from an institution. For girls, the purpose of education was to raise them to be obedient, faithful wives and to raise their children as good Christians, this purpose was no different regardless of class. Girls and boys were both taught general deportment and good behaviour. Social education was just as important for the lower classes as it was for the aristocracy.

Those who could not be spared at home would remain there until married or be sent to another household to serve in their early teens, lessening the financial burden on their family. Girls would be taught to run the household, look after children, manage servants and could often read but not many were taught to write. They would certainly learn to sew from a young age, practising different stitches on a sampler but unlikely had access to books of the more extravagant patterns that the wealthier girls would have had. It might sound cruel to us now that young girls might be sent away to another household but these households were often of a higher class than their home and provided opportunities for girls to better themselves whilst providing bed and board with a small wage. Working within a wealthier household could also provide the possibility of access to books, whether for academic purposes or practical skills and girls could work with finer materials they might not have otherwise had the opportunity to do. The master of the household would often provide a marriage dowry for female servants when a father could not. Those who married a merchant or tradesman might have then learnt to write in order to assist their husband in running the business and providing updates to their husband when he was away.

Some children of yeomen and merchants, whilst not technically aristocracy were wealthier than the majority of the lower classes and had the privilege of attending school or being tutored at home. For those residing in the country, they might be sent to a larger town or city to board at a grammar school. The majority of children were those with parents with little wealth, children of labourers, husbandmen or some yeomen. Some as noted, received no education at all whilst others would be taught in their local parish, usually by the parish priest or a schoolmaster retained by a wealthy individual for the purpose of teaching the parish children. The children would be taught their ABC, some Latin so they could learn their prayers and where possible, basic arithmetic. The number of children to receive this basic education increased in 1529 when the Convocation of Canterbury ordered every parish priest to teach the parish children to read and write when they were not busy with their religious duties.

Once at school, whether at a petty school or a grammar school, reading would be taught first. In grammar schools where it was not a prerequisite for entry, the skill of reading was taught to those who had not attended a petty school and had not been taught the skill beforehand. Reading was practiced by printed letters or reading exercises displayed on the hornbook. Children would begin with the alphabet but as they progressed would advance to words then phrases and other exercises. The first aim was for children to learn the Ava Maria and the Paternoster. Children were taught to recite the alphabet whilst their tutor pointed to each letter. The alphabet became known as the criss-cross row as it began with a cross and often followed with the rhyme 'Christ's cross be my speede, In all virtue to proceede'. After the alphabet, the first thing a child likely learnt to read was the Lord's Prayer. Most elementary schools would conduct lessons orally as they did not have the means to provide books even once the printing presses were churning out textbooks, the cost to produce books specifically for children remained high and therefore a hornbook, commonplace book and psalter were likely the most used within elementary and grammar schools. When learning to write children of the lower classes would use slate or trace letters into sand. Most would learn to write in what is known as 'secretary hand', a legible font as opposed to the swirling italic preferred by humanists.

As the importance of education increased, more children of the poorer classes were given the opportunity to receive a formal education. The parish clergy would likely have attended a grammar school as Latin was essential to their vocation, in fact, they should have been examined before receiving a benefice but this was often overlooked. This did mean that in places with no school the parish priest was often asked to teach the local children, sometimes with inducements of a house to teach from, or payments from parents who could afford to contribute. These children might at least learn Latin from someone who had received a grammar school education even if they had not continued with their education to degree level. Licenses were also granted by bishops to laymen to teach children particularly in areas where there was no school or appropriate person to teach at the church. These men would be tasked with the basic teaching of the ABC and reading. If their skill allowed, they could also teach the children to write and possibly some basic Latin along with rudimentary arithmetic.

The first aim of the grammar school was to ensure the boys understood the basic rules of Latin grammar, this would be taught through the study of Latin texts but for those without a commonplace book, they would have to learn the rules and Latin phrases by memory. Once the rudimentary rules of grammar had been mastered the boys could advance to using words together to compose prose and verse. The schoolmaster would set exercises of writing prose in Latin which would be viewed by the whole class. If the boys could compose sentences and small phrases, they could also attempt translations. There were various books compiled of collections of Latin dialogues to assist with this aspect. These texts were known as 'vulgaria' and were intended to teach children the rudiments of grammar through which children could practice their Latin composition through translating the sentences or passages from English to Latin. The vulgaria books grew more sophisticated during the period as the preference moved away from colloquial Latin towards the more elegant ancient style favoured by humanists. The vulgaria also differed in their compilation, some appeared to be dialogues altogether in no particular order whilst others like that of Horman ordered the dialogues into subject topics such as food and drink, games and family.[2] Those who could afford a copy likely had their own whilst those who could not afford to purchase one might have learnt from the schoolmaster's copy or relied on the schoolmaster to either use their copy to provide instruction or write their own dialogues for the pupils. Using these collections of dialogues was hoped to assist children to learn to speak Latin as they practiced translating passages on everyday conversation into Latin. The topics were all those that a boy would be familiar with including the study of Latin with indications of relevant authors:

The begynnynge of gramer doth well with the, for thou haste thy groundys well and ornately. Goo to it styll; tho shalte overcum it, for the begynnynge of every thynge is the hardiste, the which if a man can well he shall lightly overcum that fouleth. And therfor methynke it was a noble sayng of Aristotle: Begynnynge is more than halfe the worke.[3]

Using the vulgaria was not the only method of teaching the boys to speak Latin, they were expected to progress with the aid of the tutors requesting the boys speak Latin whilst at school and as their fluency increased, they were to be tasked with disputations, a method which would assist those who wished to progress to university and study logic. Once grammar was mastered boys could continue their studies by reading Latin authors which would also enable them to learn other subjects including history, poetry and of course, virtue and morality which remained of great importance. The most common authors would have been the same as those recommended to the aristocracy; Cicero, Horace, Virgil, Ovid and Terence amongst others.

Schools were founded by wealthy patrons and offered a number of placements free of charge to those without the means to pay. St Paul's School, London was founded in 1509 by John Colet, Dean of St Paul's. The school provided free placements for 153 boys where, if they could be spared by their families, they could expect to follow a strict regime. There were set times for waking, prayers, studies, bedtime and during out of school hours the boys were instructed by the chaplain. Colet compiled a catechism for the pupils which included English and Latin version of prayers as well as advice on behaviour down to the smallest detail such as washing and dressing.[4] The basic textbook at the school was *Æditio*, a text written in English which combined numerous works by Colet and Lily amongst others.[5] As well as being tutored in religion the boys would also receive tuition in grammar with the assistance of William Lily's grammar.

Lily was appointed by Colet as the first high master of the school and his grammar remained in use for many years. Within the statutes Colet stated:

> I would they were taught always in good literature bothe Laten and Greke, and good autors such as have the verrye Romayne eloquence joined with wisdom, specially Christen autors that wrote theire wisdom with clean and chast Laten, other in verse or in prose, for my intent is by this Scole specially to increase knowledge and worshipping of God and our Lord Christ Jesu, and good Christen life and maners in the Children. And for that entent I will the Children learne first above all the Catechizon in Englishe and after the Accidens, that I made, or some other, yt any be better to the purpose, to induce Children more spedely to laten speeche.[6]

Colet essentially wished the boys to be tutored in Latin and Greek using chaste Christian authors and to study the ancient Latin and Greek authors as well as read works of poetry. The curriculum included a variety of classical and modern authors from an elementary level through to more advanced readers. Colet recommended the classics of Aesop's *Fables* and Lucian's *Dialogues* for elementary readers whilst the comedies of Terence were included for learning the art of conversation. Cicero was included in the curriculum for philosophy and literary prose. Poetry and history were also included in Colet's curriculum with Virgil's *Aenid* and *Eclogues* being promoted along with Ovid's *Metamorphoses* and the *Epistles* of Horace for the study of poetry. History included Caesar's *Commentaries* and Sallust's *Historiae*. The central modern works of the curriculum were the *Colloquies* of Erasmus as well as his *Institutio Christiani Hominis* written especially for the school and Baptista Mantuan's *Eclogues*. It was certainly a humanist curriculum that would go on to influence numerous schools around the country. As with the majority of the schools during the period, St Paul's had one large room in which all pupils were taught. However, unlike some schools whose pupils were all taught together regardless of age and capability, St Paul's classroom was separated into four smaller areas using curtains. On visiting the school, Erasmus wrote:

> There is an entrance examination; no boy admitted who cannot read and write. The scholars are in four classes, a compartment in the school-room for each. Above the head-master's chair is a picture of the child Christ in the act of teaching; the Father in the air above, with a scroll saying 'Hear ye Him.' These words were introduced at my suggestion. The boys salute and sing a hymn on entering and leaving.[7]

Many of the boys attending grammar schools were from the wealthier families of the common classes and their education would more closely fit with that of the aristocracy without the private tutor. By the end of the Tudor period, the grammar schools were attended largely by the gentry as education became more fashionable and a way to advance. For schools that did not provide free places for poor boys, there was the opportunity to pay for their lessons by cleaning the classrooms, as well as receiving free tuition these boys might also have been provided with a uniform if the school in question did have one. Regardless of a boy's class or wealth, all were subject to the threat of corporal punishment. Schoolmasters would use a birch rod to punish boys though not all agreed with this practice. Erasmus, Vives and Ascham were all against corporal punishment and believed boys should be issued with a warning first and that learning should be an enjoyable experience.

For many boys, grammar school, whilst still a privilege, would be the final step in their education but for others, it was a stepping stone in their career or scholarship. For the majority, they would leave grammar school around the age of fourteen but some stayed longer with eighteen being the limit. There were no rules stopping common pupils from attending university particularly if they could afford the fees or were intended for the church at which point the church or monastery they were intended for would incur the fees of their education, unless they had the benefit of a wealthy patron. Before the Renaissance, men of the Church were the largest body of pupils at university and the majority were not wealthy. As with the grammar schools, if a boy could not afford the fees, he might be able to pay his way by completing chores including serving in the halls or cleaning, reducing the time available for studies but the poorer students were those most likely to come away with a degree. With the increase in wealthy pupils attending university, it actually helped to increase opportunities for poorer scholars as they were able to find employment as a servant to a wealthy pupil and therefore work their way through their degree. Some colleges enforced a requirement of residency and if employed as a servant this meant the cost of their accommodation was met by their master. Some of the most renowned scholars of the period were of humble birth.

As the Renaissance reached England many began to study the classic authors and introduce them into schools and universities. One of the first men in England to introduce work based on the classics and the new grammars coming from Italy was John Anwykyll who was appointed as headmaster of Magdalen College, Oxford a few years prior to the Tudor reign beginning. Anywykyll had studied at Cambridge in the 1470s. He is the likely author of the treatise *Compodium totius Grammatical* which was published in 1483 and was based on the works of the new Italian humanist grammarians Lorenzo Valla and Niccolo Perotti, and cited a number of classical authors including Cicero, Horace, Virgil and Quintilian. There is little doubt this work was a step in English education towards a change in the way grammar was studied. Another man of humble birth who became an excellent scholar was Thomas Wolsey. His father had been a butcher. Thomas Wolsey enrolled at Magdalen College, Oxford at the age of eleven, this was younger than usual but an exceptional achievement for someone not of the higher classes. He would later become a cardinal and Lord Chancellor and would found a school himself in Ipswich.

A further opportunity presented itself during the period for those residing in the vicinity of the university colleges when some colleges took steps to begin delivering lectures to the public and all could attend. Corpus Christi, Oxford was one of these colleges and began to deliver public lectures in Greek and Latin whilst Cardinal Thomas Wolsey intended Cardinal College, Oxford to start delivering public lectures in theology, law, philosophy and medicine.[8] Public lectures in mathematics and geometry also began in London and enabled the general public to learn about the application of calculations. For the poor who did attend university, their curriculum was much the same as that of the aristocracy, they might not have allowances for the tutor to hold and likely spent much less time enjoying pastimes as their contemporaries but they studied the same topics for the most part, the difference being that for these scholars, they intended to obtain their degree so likely spent free time studying further material. Although theology was known to be the highest of the arts there was an opportunity to study it without attending university. There were institutions open to the public dedicated to the study of theology. The first of these was the Guildhall Library in London which opened early in the fifteenth century. The Guildhall was managed by priests and held a chained library which was used by the public as well as the clergy. The Guildhall did not survive the Reformation but by that point, other public libraries had begun to open.

Many men of the Church attended university and became philosophers and theologians as well as accepting appointments within the government, in particular in the early part of the Tudor period as they were the most highly educated group of people. The dissolution of the monasteries meant many schools supported by monasteries and the chantry schools were closed, those which were saved and refounded by one of the monarchs or other means were more likely to be grammar schools rather than elementary schools and this meant the poor were the most affected. The grammar schools that were saved also began to exclude poor pupils as they were refounded with the purpose of profit for the founder by charging all pupils to attend.

Most professions were closed to women, they could not attend university although there is some evidence of few girls attending grammar schools and they could not enter the Inns of Court. Regardless of this, girls were very skilled in managing households and servants and were often knowledgeable in brewing, baking, dairies and using herbs for medicinal benefits. Knowledge of herbal remedies was passed down the generations from mother to daughter and had to be learnt by practice in those who were not literate. Girls would learn to identify herbs, when to collect them and how to make syrups, candies and tinctures using them. They could of course also take holy vows and become a nun.

Although the opportunities for education were increasing throughout the period, most people learnt through employment. Apprenticeships, although mostly incurring a cost, were an alternative to school but still provided an education and the possibility of a trade and could be formal or informal. Children of craftsmen, yeomen and even sons of the gentry, who did not have wealth and who could not afford school fees, were often apprenticed out to others rather than being taught their father's trade. The majority of trades, especially those in London and the larger towns, had a guild, which concerned themselves with setting standards for entry into the respective trades. Apprentices were available in a variety of trades from carpentry and stonemasonry to merchants and goldsmiths. Entry was usually at the age of fourteen until approximately twenty-one, the entry age suggesting some education was a pre-requisite and many of the guilds actually insisted on it within their statutes, whereas others placed the onus on the masters to ensure the apprentice was given the time to attend grammar school. One of the guilds which insisted on apprentices learning to read and write was that of the goldsmiths who added the requirement to their ordinance in 1498. The guild of scriveners was even stricter and insisted their apprentices had mastered grammar, a requirement for their trade in writing and copying. The ordinance of 1498 stated they should be 'completely erudite and learned in the books of the Parvula, genders, declensions, preterites and supines, Equivoca and synonyms, with other petty books'.[9] The guilds governed prices, wages and the training of apprentices. An apprenticeship was not an easy route and most had to serve at least seven years depending on the trade. The apprentice would join their master in their teenage years and live with their master and his family, but was not treated as a family member, more like a servant. The larger guilds often employed a chaplain to educate the members' children as well as conduct services in the guild chapel and members could use this to their advantage by sending their apprentice to learn from the chaplain. If they completed their apprenticeship to a satisfactory level, they could remain with their master as a journeyman and work for a small wage without supervision and eventually could apply to the council of their guild to be admitted and start their own business. Through an apprenticeship, especially one supervised by a reputable guild of one of the more established trades, apprentices, like their aristocratic counterparts, would not only learn the relevant skills of their chosen trade but also manners and morals.

One apprenticeship that wasn't as regulated as the crafts guilds was drama. A boy could become the apprentice of an actor and would learn the trade as well have the opportunity to play the part of children and women as it was frowned upon for females to act. Apprenticeships to actors differed from those offered by the Boys Companies which included the Children of the Chapel Royal as these boys were receiving an academic education as well as playing parts in plays. There were of course apprenticeships available in the countryside and smaller towns that might not be connected to a guild. These apprenticeships followed the same kind of rules but the apprentice might be taken on without a fee, especially in small towns, and it is probable the poorer apprentices did not acquire the literacy skills of those supervised by a guild. These opportunities allowed craftsmen and husbandmen to obtain labour while a child could learn a trade as they worked.

Under an apprenticeship, the master would teach their craft, how to run a business and also the valuable lesson of good manners. Girls could be taken on as an apprentice but most were taught at home if they did not attend a petty school. The main apprenticeship available for girls was with the Silk Women. The Silk Women were skilled in making ribbons, trimmings and tassels as well as laundering and mending clothing. The apprenticeship would last seven years and the girls would not only be taught the craft but also how to run their own business with the aim of opening their own once they had the experience to do so.[10] Apprenticeships became more regulated under the Tudors with the introduction of the Statute of Labour in 1562 which aimed to improve the standard of training provided under an apprenticeship.[11] The spread of printed material assisted apprentices as manuals on skills began to increase in availability, a master might be able to provide books or pamphlets on architecture for the mason apprentice and mathematics for the merchant apprentice. Of course, this would require the apprentice to be able to read but as noted the majority of the larger guilds required literacy upon the beginning of an apprenticeship.

For the poorest children, neither school nor an apprenticeship were options. Children of the poorest members of society were set to work at an early age, did not attend school and were largely illiterate. To send a child to school sacrificed the availability of their labour at home, which for some was not a viable option. Location also hindered education, wider opportunities were available in larger towns and cities, particularly London but for those in the country, there was often no school nearby. For these children, education meant learning through work, as young as seven they would begin working at home. For boys this might mean working in the fields whilst for girls it would mean assisting with looking after the home and where present, maintaining the animals and collection of produce for the family. If a child was lucky, they might be able to obtain a position in a wealthier household but they would still be set to work. In some areas, the parish might take on the responsibility and cost of teaching young poor children a craft such as spinning but not all towns and villages had the wealth to be able to afford to do this. The poor had little requirement for literacy as it was unlikely, they would need to write or prepare accounts and would get by with learning their prayers by memory. If there was a local petty school that could be attended free, a poor child might be able to attend for a couple of years and learn basic reading and psalms but attendance would depend on the need of their family to allow them the time to attend, often making attendance inconsistent.

Although most of the educational opportunities discussed have been for children, there were adult pupils who attended grammar schools. They would have to sit with children but were mostly traders and merchants whose increase in wealth now allowed them to attend a grammar school to learn to read and write. Professional writers known as scriveners were employed to document accounts, draft wills and letters and some offered private schools where they would teach writing to merchants, traders and some clergy. During this period professions began to keep records of transactions, stock and other correspondence. This also provided a large inducement to learn to read and write. The wealthier also sought positions within their local community, these positions including bailiffs, members of parliament and tax collectors would require literacy skills so the effort of learning even as an adult was well worth the benefit if a position was obtained especially as this could begin the climb up the social ladder to a position at court. In the fifteenth century, paper was replacing parchment and was a much cheaper alternative resulting in increased demand to learn to write and it could be taught for a lower fee as scriveners could teach their pupils using paper rather than wasting costly parchment. This was also an option for children who might not be able to afford or travel to a grammar school but had a scrivener nearby who could teach them to write.

Although the education of common people was affected by the Reformation and the closure of monastic and chantry schools, the quality of the education seemingly improved under the Tudors. Henry VIII attempted to regulate and improve the quality of education and in 1540 authorised the use of the Royal Grammar, which had been written by William Lily originally for St Paul's School in 1510. This became the approved Latin grammar to be used in all schools, meaning those in less affluent schools would be taught using the same grammar as their contemporaries in wealthier schools. This uniform Latin grammar was followed by an elementary grammar in 1542 and finally a children's primer in 1545.

The largest influence on education for common people was actually commoners in the form of merchants. These men had become increasingly wealthy and a vast number of schools were founded by wealthy patrons in their local towns. Some endowed schools to show their wealth whilst others genuinely wished to help improve the opportunities for boys in the community. Some merchants would pay for a house with a schoolmaster to teach local boys, others would pay for the building of a whole school and the provision of schoolmasters and study materials. These schools not only provided education for local boys but also provided literate apprentices for men in the vicinity, a boy would likely be more successful in obtaining an apprenticeship if he could read and write, especially as the master would not then need to pay for his schooling. The extremely wealthy even founded grammar schools and implemented statutes, such as St Paul's, these statutes provided not only the rules for how the schools should be run but usually included a provision for the education of a number of 'poor boys' and the curriculum to be taught. As for the colleges, new ones were founded and scholarships were awarded through the donations of benefactors or the Church which allowed some poor boys to receive a thorough formal education even up to the level of a Master's degree or doctorate. It is likely that without the wealthy benefactors who founded petty and grammar schools across England and endowed scholarships at colleges, the poor people of the lower classes would have been waiting much longer for educational opportunities and even with all the foundations, not all poor children were lucky enough to receive any formal education at all. It is apparent that although education increased in importance under the Tudors and certainly improved among the higher levels, elementary education remained the most unorganised with no specific textbooks or curriculum. It is this level of education that most of the common children of the poorer classes would have benefited from but unfortunately, it was the last to receive attention and certainly did not achieve the patronage of the higher educational establishments.

Chapter Seven

Religion as Education

The Tudors lived in a time when religion was central to culture and moral sanctions were feared. All were conscious of whether their actions would have consequences after their death and therefore took their moral responsibility and piety seriously. The Tudors also needed to avoid being accused of heresy which carried a sentence of being burned to death, so it is easy to understand why religious education from an early age was important, regardless of a person's class or gender. Thomas Aquinas was a thirteenth-century Dominican Friar, Doctor of the Church and philosopher who believed that children needed grace to reach divine knowledge and their full potential whilst Aristotle stated that a child's mind was like a blank page and they needed to be taught to be virtuous and should be encouraged from as early as possible.

At the beginning of the period, learning was mostly to be devoted to the service of God. The central aim of education was to improve the standard of piety and provide a society of good Christians. Everyone wished to avoid or reduce the time spent in purgatory. Purgatory was the destination between heaven and hell, those without sin would go straight to heaven whilst those who had sinned but not enough to go to hell would spend time in purgatory. It was hoped prayer, piety and good deeds would reduce the time spent in purgatory. For the wealthy, this also meant they had the means to bequeath funds for prayers to be said for their souls after their death and might leave instructions in their will for bequests to be made to churches. Some gifts were made in the hopes of reducing time spent in purgatory.

It was a mother's duty to begin the education of her children in religion and this education began early with children being encouraged to walk rather than crawl as crawling was seen as un-Christian. The wealthy would use something similar to today's baby walker and push toys. Although women were responsible for the early religious education of their children, they were forbidden to have positions within the Church and could not be ordained. The mother's own literacy levels would determine the education received by her children. For those of the wealthy classes, it was likely the mother could speak and read Latin which would assist them in learning to read prayers whereas the lowers classes would have to rely on prayers learnt by rote from their parents or through attendance at church often without understanding the meaning of the words they recited, at least until prayers began to be said in the vernacular. If a woman did not wish to marry, entering into a life of religion was the main career path as almost all others were closed to females. Nunneries also provided education for girls and provided opportunities for earning responsibility as well as studying. The extent to which girls could progress also depended on their social class, lower classes could not hope to achieve the role of an abbess and could usually only reach the level of a lay sister whilst wealthier girls could reach higher levels of responsibility and were often less restricted within the nunneries.

Religion was not just observance but formed part of daily life and religious education took many forms. All children were taught that on waking, their first thoughts should be of God, and their first words should be about God. Morning prayers remained an essential part of the daily routine for all classes and continued after the Reformation. Children would learn to recite psalms in Latin at least up to the Reformation and most children had to learn these by rote as many did not have the means to afford books or manuscripts. Not everyone was equally pious but religious observances affected all aspects of daily life. The Church also held some responsibility for the religious education of children. Through attendance at a house of worship, children would learn how to behave in church, how to worship and about Christian ethics. These behaviours would be encouraged outside of church as well to ensure children grew up with a code of piety and virtue. Confession formed a large part of the Catholic faith but in order to make confession, a person must know what constitutes sin. That was the role of the parish or household priest, to educate children in the sacrament of penance and for the parents to ensure the continuation and adherence of these lessons outside of church.

A tract produced at the time gives the advice; 'wash your hands and wrists, your face, and eyes, and your teeth, with cold water, and after that you be apparelled, walk in your garden or park, a thousand pace or two. And then great and noble men doth use to hear mass'.[1] Henry VIII would hear Mass every morning, either in his private chapel or if it was a Sunday or other holy day, he would go to the palace chapel and celebrate with pomp with courtiers, chaplains and the choir of the Chapel Royal. The alphabet was the first thing a child learnt to read and even that had religious bearings. Children would make the cross and say 'Christ's cross me speed' before beginning to recite their ABC.[2] After they had learnt their ABC, they would progress to learning the Paternoster by spelling it out, before moving on to Ave Maria, the Creed and the Ten Commandments, all of which they would be expected to be able to recite either from memory or using their own prayer book. At the start of the Tudor reign, these would all be recited in Latin but by the time Edward VI ascended to the throne they were in English.

Schools were initially founded with the aim of producing educated clergy so they could understand the Christian doctrines and further the Christian religion. The clergy and those of religious orders were tasked with learning the scriptures and doctrines so they had the ability to carry out religious observances correctly and also pass on their knowledge through divine services and teaching. For those children lucky enough to receive a formal education at school, religion would become the forefront of their learning. The majority of schools would begin and end the day with prayers which continued after the Reformation. The more elementary schools would teach the most common prayers whilst grammar schools would implement a more regimented regime. All elementary schools, including petty schools and almonry schools, taught the ABC before moving on to the primer and catechism. The more affluent elementary establishments were able to advance to further religious education including the psalter and the Testaments. Elementary education signalled the importance of religion whilst also providing a beginning in literacy skills.

Song schools were of great importance for elementary religious education. Boys were taught to study plainsong which was the reciting of psalms and hymns. The benefit of learning song was that the boys would learn to speak Latin with perfect pronunciation. Many would not at first understand the words they were reciting but in due course could begin to learn their meaning and if songbooks were used could also begin to learn to write through copying the text. Books were not always available and songs had to be learnt by rote therefore offering little chance of learning to write unless a priest or master was willing to provide tuition to the boys aside from the study of song. The wealthier song schools such as those supported by the cathedrals would have provided much more opportunities for boys to learn to read and write and the additional possibility of performing in the cathedral choir. As the nobility and royal family had choirs in their homes, the cathedral choirs were ideal for those wishing to recruit new choir boys.

Of the elementary schools before the Reformation, chantry schools provided the best religious instruction. Chantry priests had no other responsibilities other than to say Masses for the benefactor of the chantry chapel and therefore had more time to educate children. They were also usually educated themselves in Latin and grammar and in some cases to degree level including degrees in the higher art of theology. Chantry priests could often provide more than simple prayers and could usually read the scriptures with the children, a much more advanced curriculum than that of other elementary establishments. For those intended for a career in the Church, education at a chantry school was free, the basic curriculum being reading and spelling and often the study of song to assist the priest in celebrating Mass but any advancement on this depended on the skills of the chantry priest. Those schools endowed by a beneficiary such as a wealthy merchant could also provide education to the poor children of the local community and could accept other children for a fee. Some of the university colleges would support chantry and song schools as this enabled them to call upon the boys to assist in the celebration of Mass.

The boys who attended boarding schools also found religion at the centre of their education. They would be subject to prayers at specific times including the reciting of prayers whilst making their beds. On Sundays and other religious festivities, the pupils of boarding schools might be expected to walk from school to the chapel in an orderly form whilst reciting psalms. If they had not already learnt them before arriving at school, the boys would be expected to learn by heart the Ten Commandments, Ava Maria (prior to the Reformation at least) and the Apostle's Creed. Some schools would also teach children the seven sins and the seven sacraments; confession, eucharist, penance, baptism, holy orders, marriage and anointing the sick. From 1536, parishes were obliged to teach local children basic reading skills and instruction in religion, in poorer areas these lessons often had to take place within the parish church as there was no school present. The established schools and attendance at church were not the only methods of obtaining religious education, many villages and individuals employed a tutor to provide religious instruction to children. This could take place in a home or church and sometimes the tutor would be provided with his own home with the stipulation he had to teach the local children. Parish clerks, priests and chaplains also took on the responsibility for educating local children on an informal basis, some for little or no payment but as a result of a belief that it was their moral duty to do so. The parish clerks would mostly train boys in song and how they could serve the parish priest at Mass whilst the priest would undertake the academic education. It is likely however that in some areas the clerk would take on more responsibility and provide the best education he could to local children. In the countryside, a lack of schools possibly led to much informal education delivered by men of the Church who sought to instil piety into children and by those who believed education was valuable for all.

In the absence of elementary school textbooks, prayer books acted as both religious guidance and learning aids. All religious houses along with men of the Church and laity owned copies of the psalter and matins book which could be used by children to practice their reading skills and if they aimed to learn to write could be the ideal starting point to begin copying letters from after the alphabet. If a boy was intended for further study, he could begin the study of the texts in Latin as well as English which would make their progression to a grammar school much easier especially as during the period many implemented statutes required varying degrees of literacy upon entry. Those who went on to attend grammar school would be taught the usual trivium and at an advanced level the quadrivium which would include religious aspects of calculations that determined the Church calendar, the movement of celestial bodies and the rules of plainsong.

At local fayres and church events, priests made use of puppet shows to teach passages from the Bible and religious stories. The puppet show provided a form of entertainment as well as education, particularly for the illiterate members of the congregation. Songs and plays performed at fayres would have a religious theme, meaning children learnt even when having fun and for adults, they would be reminded of their religious responsibilities on a regular basis. Religious education did not end with childhood and adults continued to learn through religious literature and attendance at religious services along with participation in pastimes. One of the most enjoyable forms of religious instruction was the cycle of mystery plays. These plays were performed by guild members and each performance would tell a different biblical story. In the larger towns, this could take all day and would be performed as part of a pageant from atop wagons so spectators could remain in one place and watch as each wagon stopped, performed then moved on and the next would begin. The Feast of Corpus Christi which celebrates the Eucharist falls in May or June and was the most popular time or the cycle of mystery plays.[3] The day usually began with the celebration of Mass, followed by the blessed sacrament being carried through the streets to the church in a procession of ecclesiastical figures and guilds. Once the more formal events had ended the entertainment could begin. Observers would benefit from scenes of the Last Judgement, Adam and Eve and other biblical stories. It was not only the guilds that would stage plays, churches up to the Reformation would sometimes present a play during services. Some were performed in Latin and were most common at Easter and Christmas, the Church aiming to provide instruction in aspects of worship and personal devotion, others were in English and told the stories of saints.[4] Another social aspect of religious life was the parish guilds. These were set up to help the parish priest and church with activities in the community. The guilds would dedicate prayers to those in need of aid or for the souls of members of the guild. They would also organise pageants and processions with religious themes with funds being used for the upkeep of the church or for the poor in the local community. Wealthy parish guilds would support schools and hospitals as well as any upkeep of the community such as roads or community buildings. Members were expected to behave with decorum and act as peacekeepers if required during disputes. Guild members were required to pay a fee to join and annual dues, making them more enticing to the wealthy who might have viewed the good deeds of the guild as a way to assist their own soul when they passed and be comforted in the knowledge the guild would pray for their soul.

For a boy intended for the Church or religious house, he could expect to attend grammar school for at least five years before he could take holy orders. Candidates for holy orders had to be eighteen before they could be made sub-deacons so most took the opportunity to continue their education up until this point, others might assist tutors in teaching to pass the time until they became of age. Twenty was the minimum age to become a deacon. These young men could be ordained by the bishop if they were thought to have accomplished the learning expected of them but others might be asked to continue their education for a further period before they could progress any further within the Church hierarchy. Those wishing to enter the Church required knowledge of Latin. All members of the clergy were expected to observe the divine office; the eight daily services to God, and dependent on their role within the church would also be required to complete services including Mass, baptism and marriage. For all of these, the ability to read and speak Latin was essential and in 1530 the convocation of Canterbury ordered that all members of the clergy were to study the scriptures or texts by one of the fathers of the church for a number of hours each week.[5] Those seeking to climb the ladder in the Church might need to seek further education as some offices such as Bishops might be called upon to act in legal disputes or diplomatic missions. Those of high office within the Church often took education seriously and were responsible for the foundation or endowment of schools and colleges, some of which remain today. Corpus Christi College, Oxford was founded in 1517 by Bishop Fox who favoured the humanist curriculum and intended the college to provide renaissance learning to England's scholars. The college statutes included reference to a curriculum of both Latin and Greek texts and even included authors to be studied. Fox intended Cicero, Sallust, Pliny, Livy, Virgil, Ovid and Terence to form the basis of the Latin authors whilst Plutarch, Euripides, Aristotle, Demosthenes, Thucydides and Sophocles were included as the Greek authors. Cardinal Thomas Wolsey founded Cardinal College, Oxford in 1525 which is now known as Christ's Church, Oxford after it was refounded by Henry VIII following the fall of Wolsey.[6]

The founding of establishments was not the only way those in office encouraged education, they were also patrons of scholars, as we have seen Cardinal Morton was a patron of Thomas More but Erasmus also found a patron in the Archbishop of Canterbury, William Warham. Even with the increase in humanist favoured curriculums within schools and the university colleges, the seven liberal arts remained important to men of the Church, or at least some did. Grammar was required in order to read religious writings but decreased in colleges as it was seen as more important to school education, the last degree in Latin grammar being awarded in 1569 at Oxford. Astronomy for determining dates of religious holidays such as Easter remained an important part of the curriculum, dialectic was useful for debate and rhetoric enabled men to compose sermons. Astrology began to attract religious scholars as they sought to examine how heavenly bodies interacted with the rest of the world. It also influenced the study of medicine, as noted in Chapter Six, medicine was based on the four humours and scholars believed horoscopes affected these humours, therefore it was not just medical students that studied astrology but also churchmen including those at the monasteries. Those wishing to enter a monastery would usually follow the initial path of other boys, they might not attend a grammar school and instead be taught in a monastic school. Novices were usually around the age of twenty when admitted to a monastery giving the young men much opportunity to attend university after school and continue their studies. Even after admittance novices would often spend additional years studying grammar and logic either at university or within the monastery and many studied the higher art of theology or began producing their own writings or translations of texts.

Even after the Reformation, religion remained a dominant influence on university colleges. From 1536 students were required to undertake the Oath of Supremacy and all students were expected to attend the college chapel. Theology and Hebrew were noted as compulsory subjects for completion of a Master of Arts and were often taught by senior members of the colleges who also happened to be members of the clergy. The universities continued to provide educated clergy, but the focus of education shifted away from grammar to intellectual teachings of Latin and Greek classical authors. The Reformation did result in Catholics being unable to attend university due to the requirement of renouncing Rome, unless of course they took the oath and attended anyway. This did not mean their education ceased, there remained Catholic tutors who would teach Catholic children and of course, the monks and chantry priests found alternative employment in teaching. Some university colleges were well aware that Catholics still enrolled and provided them with a Catholic tutor, some even housed them together away from other students.[7]

Formal education was not the only form of religious education, attending church was important to all but personal devotions were just as important and also formed part of an individual's education. Literature to aid personal devotion was available, more so with the introduction of the printing press. A large number of wealthy individuals owned a Book of Hours which was effectively a personal prayer book. A Book of Hours was usually handwritten by scribes or monks and could be highly illuminated meaning they were expensive but were available with minimal illumination. These books were based on the Divine Office and contained the Little Office of the Blessed Virgin Mary, which provided shorter versions of the services in the Divine Office. The services are the devotions to be made during the eight canonical hours from Matins to Compline, the rest of the contents differed but most contained a calendar of Church feast days, texts, psalms, hymns, extracts from the Gospels and masses from major feast days. The books could be personalised and many would add important dates such as births to their own books along with annotations and additional texts. They were efficient in providing a routine for religious observances as well as reading matter for the pious. Books of Hours were often bequeathed in wills of the wealthy to family members. Lady Margaret Beaufort bequeathed one of her Book of Hours to Westminster Abbey. A complete collection of psalms could be purchased in a psalter, another popular choice for personal devotions.

Other guides to worship and personal devotion could be found everywhere, on the walls in the form of tapestries and in manuscripts and scrolls such as the scroll given by Henry to William Thomas, noted in Chapter Two. The illuminations were to provide a guide to devotions: The first illumination of the Trinity was accompanied by the Latin prayer of victory over enemies. The second was an illumination of the crucifixion which formed the core of Christianity. Those viewing the image were instructed to take in the image in detail, considering the Five Wounds and pray as they did so. Further instructions were provided including which psalms to chant and when prayers should be said throughout the devotions. Further illuminations required a specific number of different psalms and prayers to be chanted as images were viewed. This repetition was known as 'Spiritual exercise' and was performed to improve the mind and spirit. The devout, including Henry VIII, would exercise their minds but it was not just an improvement of the mind that was believed to be of gain through spiritual exercise but also specific rewards which could be found in manuscripts including the one given by Henry to William Thomas, the main reward being a reduction in the time spent in purgatory.[8]

For the less wealthy, small prayer books or pamphlets of meditations, hymns and prayers including the Lord's Prayer could be purchased, they could also use a blank notebook and make their own book of personal devotion, adding prayers and psalms to it and any religious verses they wished to remember. The rosary also aided devotion by helping to keep track of repeated prayers or psalms. Rosaries could be very basic or exquisite and made of expensive materials. Common people looked to strange phenomena for indications on whether God was pleased with them such as storms and comets whilst the aristocracy and royalty hoped for God's endorsement in times of war and through historical accounts. For those wishing for a specific blessing or to increase their personal devotions and bring them closer to God, they could go on pilgrimage. Our Lady of Walsingham was a popular pilgrimage destination for the Tudors seeking blessing or relief for specific reasons and was visited by Henry VII, Henry VIII, Katharine of Aragon and Anne Boleyn amongst others before it was destroyed during the dissolution of the monasteries. Pilgrimage was not a requirement but was undertaken by many wishing to enhance their spiritual life or give thanks for blessings but was of course another way of expressing piety in an effort to reduce time spent in purgatory.

The Reformation is sometimes linked to humanism in that some believe it was due to the influence and teachings of humanists that caused the Reformation. However, the most influential humanists in England were Thomas More, Erasmus and Juan Luis Vives, all of whom remained Catholic. Humanism is very difficult to define as it was based on personal interpretations, religion and politics. The Renaissance did bring about interest in the writings of ancient Christian fathers such as Augustine, Origen and Cyprian. The Bible was also read much more, either by those who were now able to learn Latin, those who had been able to obtain a copy in English or scholars. For humanists, their studies of the ancient writings and the Bible were entwined, they had to learn Greek or Hebrew to be able to read the original texts and be able to understand the Bible to study the ancient works. Their aim was to study the scriptures and ancient Church fathers in their original form to understand the true meaning, translate them to Latin or English, edit and publish them. Scholars published treatises, translations, plays, poems and books such Erasmus' *Praise of Folly*. The increase in English translations did not mean that scholars or intended clergy ceased to study Latin, they just learned the classical version to better understand the writings of ancient authors.

It would be wrong to say that humanism had no impact on the Reformation. Due to the increased study of the Bible and scriptures,

Henry VIII had the perfect audience to request support for the annulment of his marriage from Katharine of Aragon after the Pope had refused to annul it. Henry VIII petitioned scholars all over Europe for their opinion of the validity of his marriage according to the Bible as he was of the opinion it was invalid due to Leviticus 20:21 'If a man takes his brother's wife, it is impurity; he has uncovered his brother's nakedness, they shall be childless'. Henry VIII believed this to mean no sons. Deuteronomy 25:5 on the other hand says 'If brothers dwell together and one of them dies and has no son, the wife of the dead shall not be remarried outside of the family to a stranger; her husband's brother shall go into her, and take her as his wife, and perform the duty of a husband's brother to her', which was exactly what had happened when Henry's brother Arthur died.

Therefore, the Renaissance brought about an increase in religious study and whilst it might have impacted the Reformation it cannot be said that it had sole responsibility. Henry VIII, whilst he relied on humanist scholars and broke with Rome, remained a Catholic. With the rediscovery of ancient texts and languages, the Bible and religious texts became the focus of many. Prior to this, scholars tended to write commentaries on the Bible but as the ancient works could now be read, scholars and men of the Church began to review the Bible in its original language and write their own translations or commentaries on the ancient writings. Understandably, some ecclesiastics were not enthusiastic about the Bible and religious texts being studied or assessed and felt the Bible should remain in its current form to only be read by men of the Church. Scholars began to deliver lectures and sermons on the words of the Bible and ancient religious texts rather than the commonly used Bible and the medieval commentaries on the writings. Prior to 1526, the Bible was only available in Latin; the New Testament was produced in English in 1526 followed by the complete Bible in 1535. The translation was the cause of dispute amongst people, some believed the Bible should be read by all whilst others believed it should only be read by those with the education to interpret it correctly. A consequence of this and the availability of other translations was the increase in scholarly debates and traditions and practices of the Church being questioned, exactly what some men of the Church were afraid of. Some felt the Church was being attacked and whilst some did seek reform, most only sought to understand the original writings and many scholars sought papal approval of their work. Some reformers felt the actual practices of the Church differed from the Bible and therefore produced translations or commentaries heavily indicating where the writing differed from actual practices. Of course, there were those who went further and did attack the Church in their writings, diminishing papal authority and encouraging all to read the scriptures for themselves rather than defer to the Pope.

In 1534, Henry VIII declared himself Supreme Head of the Church in England when he broke from Rome. Thomas Cranmer produced the Ten Articles in 1536 which were the first guidelines of the Church of England. Purgatory was denied but the majority of tradition was maintained with the Ten Commandments, Paternoster and Ave Maria being instructed to be taught in English rather than Latin. Most of the religious observances remained the same with few changes but one major change was the use of an English Bible in 1539 which was to be used in every church, allowing everyone to understand its contents. Before this, only those who could read and speak Latin could study the Bible, and those who couldn't had no option other than to rely on priests or educated parties to explain it to them. The lower social classes learnt prayers by memory but did not necessarily understand what they were actually saying.

A statute of 1542-3 forbade women and specific classes, including those under the class of husbandmen and labourers, from reading the Bible as it was feared those in these classes would begin to study the Bible and as a result might interpret it incorrectly. Edward VI, on the other hand, ensured the Bible was available to all. This freedom did not succeed under Mary I who halted the printing until Elizabeth succeeded to the throne and once again made the Bible available to all.[9] The dissolution of the monasteries occurred between 1536 and 1540 and would have impacted education, especially those who attended establishments connected to monasteries, this would have included the monks themselves who would study in the monastery libraries. Many moved to secular establishments whilst others had no option and lost their homes as well as their educational opportunities.

In 1545, a new prayer book was introduced with all references to the Pope removed and in 1549 the *Book of Common Prayer*, written by Archbishop Thomas Cranmer set out church services in English for the first time. The same year it was made illegal to use Catholic forms of worship. Between 1549 and 1553 saw the suppression of the chantries which again impacted those being educated at religious houses, this time those at chantry schools. Although some monks and chantries were reinstated under Mary, they did not recover to their former level. Many former monks became schoolmasters and many chapels and chantries found new use as schoolrooms. The monks that turned to teaching had the benefit of education, they were highly fluent in Latin and the scriptures and many had studied the higher faculty of theology at the universities. These benefits would be passed on to the children they taught following the Reformation. The *Geneva Bible* arrived in England in 1560 but was not printed in England until 1579, and became the most popular version until the publication of the King James Bible over fifty years later. The *Geneva Bible,* printed in English, not only provided readers with the Bible but also guides to studying the scriptures and verse citations so every reader could compare different verses. Maps, woodcuts and summaries of each book of the Bible enabled readers to study it much more effectively than previous versions had allowed.

The Reformation also meant that canon law was removed from the curriculum at both universities, degrees and teaching on the subject prohibited. This obviously impacted the clergy who had previously attended university to study the subject. The libraries of all the university colleges were purged of Catholic material and much was destroyed with pupils taught biblical theology as a replacement to scholastic theology. The clergy were not removed from their responsibilities within education and throughout the Tudor period, they remained vital to education, from priests teaching in local villages and colleges to bishops approving schoolmaster licenses. Developments in religion made reading and studying the Bible for oneself possible but also made it an ideal that people should do so, although this was not the feeling amongst all factions. For the majority, the printing press largely affected their reading of religious material. Together with an English version of the Bible, this led to many more people aiming to become literate and studying religious texts for themselves, but it was not just religion that people began to study with the increase in publications.

Each of the Tudor monarchs also had an individual influence on religious education through statutes allowing or banning people from reading the Bible to the founding of schools and approval of texts for use across the schools. For the first part of his reign, Henry VIII did little to influence education in England, leaving the control of schools to the Church and he made little attempt at first to ensure the survival or replacement of schools run or supported by the monasteries until around 1540 when he began to support the policies of founding new cathedral schools and planned to appoint readers of divinity at each. Although the plans for readers of divinity did not reach fruition his children did ensure the lectures continued at established cathedral institutions and encouraged the introduction of these lectures in new establishments. Edward VI furthered the Reformation by dissolving the chantries but he took steps to ensure many of the schools were protected. The statute for the dissolution of the chantries in 1547 included a clause that grammar schools connected to chantries would be maintained and a few new schools were endowed using chantry property, resulting in many of the King Edward VI schools present today, but the smaller elementary schools still suffered. Beginning in 1554, during the reign of Mary I, uniformity of education was further established, schoolmasters were to be examined by the bishops and if required replaced by catholic schoolmasters. From 1556 the bishops were tasked with licensing schoolmasters before they were allowed to teach to ensure they had the relevant knowledge and skills, whether this happened in all cases is doubtful but it is apparent education remained important to the Marian regime. Lastly, Elizabeth I imposed rules that schoolmasters would hold daily prayers and attend church with their pupils as well as teaching approved English or Latin catechisms. There is no doubt the Tudor monarchs were keen to improve education although much of it was due to their own religious preferences.

Chapter Eight

Books, Music & Drama

Prior to William Caxton establishing his printing press in London in 1476, most books were an expensive commodity. There were some printed books available but Caxton and the Oxford University Press certainly affected the spread of printed books. Before the introduction of the printing presses, books were created by monks and scriveners, but, as they were handwritten, took a long time to complete. The printing press introduced books to a wider audience, and whilst the majority of books were aimed at middle and upper classes, there were pamphlets printed that were aimed at the lower classes, allowing them to purchase their own reading material. Lady Margaret Beaufort, mother of Henry VII, was a patron of the printing press and she supported William Caxton, Wynkyn de Worde and Richard Pynson. One of the books commissioned by Lady Margaret Beaufort was a translation of the devotional poetry *The Miroir or Glasse of the Synneful Soul* originally written by Queen Margaret of Navarre. Pynson printed it for Lady Margaret Beaufort in 1506 after she had translated it from French to English herself, this is the same work that was later translated by Elizabeth as a gift for Katheryn Parr. Katheryn Parr was actually the first English queen to have her own work published under her own name, in English. Her *Prayers and Meditations* were published in 1545.[1]

Many of the first books were copies of the ancient manuscripts of Roman authors such as Aristotle, Plato, Cicero, Quintilian, Livy and Horace to name a few. These were mostly printed in Latin but began to be translated into the vernacular across the continent. Caxton translated devotional works himself before printing them but also printed much sought-after popular romances such as Malory's *Le Morte d'Arthur* and Chaucer's *Canterbury Tales. Le Morte d'Arthur* was originally made up of eight tales and the whole collection was called *The Whole Book of King Arthur and of His Noble Knights of the Round Table,* not a very catchy title, so when Caxton published it, he split the work into twenty-one books and gave it the much shorter title. The book includes tales ranging from how Arthur became King of Britain, the pursual of the Holy Grail, Lancelot and Guinevere and ends with Arthur going to the Vale of Avalon, tales that are still popular today. Various books were illustrated using woodcuts, a block was cut to leave a raised design which when covered in ink and pressed to paper left the illustration. The blocks could be used repeatedly and were quicker to make and use than the original method of hand-drawn illuminations, although they are perhaps not as beautiful as some of the intricate illuminations that have survived from the period.

At the end of the fifteenth century, most printed books were aimed at the wealthy or scholars as noted in Chapter One. It was not until the sixteenth century that large numbers of books began to circulate with humanist subjects being printed such as textbooks on arithmetic and grammars for Latin to assist learning such as that used in many schools. The Latin grammar written by William Lily being one such example. The first schoolbook printed in England is believed to have been the *Distichs of Cato*, which Caxton published in Latin and English in 1477 and was used throughout the whole period. Dictionaries also became available with English to Latin translations and vice versa and glossaries explaining the English meaning of Latin or French terms in specialist subjects such as law and medicine became a handy accompaniment for students who could afford them. The Renaissance brought a wealth of literature on medicine to the attention of medical scholars, over four hundred books written by Galen were discovered and translated from Greek to Latin, having a huge impact on medical studies.

The new market for books also meant that they began to appear in English rather than Latin. Initially, English books were merely translations of other books as none were written in English, but this changed as English became more popular. Many books were used as a tool to improve a person, people would read to improve their knowledge but also to improve their character by learning morality and courtesy. Cicero's *De Officiis*, written in 44 BC, takes the form of a letter from Cicero to his son and was extremely popular during the Renaissance. It contained three books, the first covered what behaviours and duties were deemed as honourable and virtuous, the second, duties which might lead to advancement and the third dealt with conflicts arising from advantages and acting honourably. *Secretum Secretorum* (The Secret of Secrets) purports to be a work written by Aristotle for his pupil Alexander the Great but was likely written in the ninth century and contains advice on a number of topics from statecraft, ethics, medicine and magic. The work was extremely popular under the Tudors, especially those with humanist interests as Aristotle became the focus of much attention amongst scholars. It was not just ancient writers that produced these books of advice but also the scholars of the day who began to produce books that became known as 'mirrors for princes', which were effectively treatises of advice for princes. Just as Skelton had written *Speculum Principis* (Mirror of the Prince) specifically for the young Henry, other writers produced books titled the same or similar to these works on courtesy as they became extremely fashionable not just amongst royalty but also the aristocracy. These books did not provide specific advice on the art of government and ruling but instead aimed to provide moral advice ensuring readers adhered to the knightly code of chivalry, something Henry VIII was keen to embrace. The most popular work in this category of books is likely to have been *Il Cortigiano,* also known as *The Book of the Courtier,* written by Baldassare Castiglione in Urbino in 1508 and published in English in 1561. Castiglione discusses what makes the ideal courtier and perfect lady through a series of dialogues. Similar to Cicero, Castiglione places great emphasis on oratory and the presentation of oneself when speaking and notes that women's intellect should not be ignored.

For females, *Miroir des Dames*, a book of moral instruction for queens and high-born noble ladies was available. Henry VII presented Elizabeth of York with an illuminated copy so it is likely her daughters Margaret, and Mary would have also read it. Vives' *De Institutione Feminae Christianae* written in 1523 for Henry VIII's daughter Mary was translated into English in 1529 by Richard Hyrde with the title *Instruction of a Christian Woman* and became the standard book for educating aristocratic females. Amongst Caxton's translations and publications was another book aimed at females, an English version of Geoffrey de la Tour Landry's *Book of the Knight of the Tower*, originally written in French during the fourteenth century by the knight as a book of moral stories for his daughters. Another, *The Book of Good Manners*, a compilation of texts based on the scriptures, was an extremely popular work amongst the lower classes. Published by Caxton, it aimed to instil manners and decorum into those especially when interacting with their social betters. Also printed by Caxton was *Book of the Ordre of Chyvalry* which he published with the aim of encouraging the aristocracy to behave in conjunction with the knightly code which he felt was declining.[2]

As merchants and yeomen became wealthier the opportunity to mix in higher social circles presented itself. Books on decorum, conversation and letter writing were a means of fitting into these circles. *The Enimie of Idleness (1568)* provided coaching in the method of writing letters and *The English Society (1586)* provided template letters for readers to copy and amend to their individual needs.[3] Merchants would also make use of books of English dialogues and polyglot dictionaries, published to learn languages. Latin was still taught in schools but if a person had not had the opportunity to attend school, they could teach themselves and could also learn other languages which might assist them in their business ventures, French being a popular choice. The number of books to learn languages increased during the period but there were few in the early years. Caxton published *Dialogues in French and English* around 1480 but

A good boke to lerne to speke French proved more popular when it was printed by Pynson and de Worde more than once before the beginning of the sixteenth century.

Other popular topics with professionals such as merchants, seamen, and surveyors were mathematics, navigation, geography and astronomy. Books on these subjects became popular as people could use them to educate themselves in accounting, plotting voyages and ship building. Although those at the court of Elizabeth I had the benefit of the knowledge of John Dee, normal adventurers were not so fortunate, therefore the publication of Anthony Ashley's *The Mariner's Mirror* in 1588 provided a wealth of advice on nautical instruction. Robert Recorde's *The Pathway to Knowledge* was published in 1551 as the first book based on geometry, printed in the English language. Edward VI had studied the book himself along with other mathematical works and it went on to become the standard textbook on geometry for decades. This was not the first book published by Recorde, he had published *The Ground of Arts* in 1543 in which he argued mathematics was necessary for all studies including law, trade and science. Humphrey Baker agreed in his 1546 publication of *The Well Spring of Science's which teacheth the perfect work and practice of Arithmetic.* There was a wealth of literature being created to assist and guide those who required calculations in their trade or studies.

Further down the social scale was the best-selling *Book of Husbandry*, published c.1523. It is believed to have been written by Sir Anthony Fitzherbert and offers a wealth of advice on farming. A large proportion of the population were husbandmen who were small landowners or free tenant farmers but this title was more than likely also read by yeoman farmers who worked for themselves and who were the next step on the social ladder from husbandmen. The reader could find advice on recognising and treating crop diseases, the best animal for ploughing and advice on how to repair highways. Husbandmen were obliged to assist in highway repairs for four days per year, rising to six before the end of the Tudor reign. The duties of the farmer's wife were also discussed, she should rise early and pray before preparing milk and breakfast, feed the animals, and make dairy products. Clothmaking and haymaking were also covered as well as knowing how to make malt. It appears the life of a farmer's wife was far from idle.[4] Further publications allowed the lower classes to learn about estate management and land surveying whilst the aristocracy would be more interested in the topics of fortification, and architecture when building their Tudor castles and manor homes.

Educational manuals were also a popular subject, providing information on what a child should learn and how they should be taught. Educational theory proved to be highly popular with books such as Thomas Elyot's *The Book Named the Governor* being reprinted at least eight times between 1531 and the 1580s.[5] *Education of a Christian Prince* written by Erasmus was presented to Henry VIII in 1517 with a covering letter complimenting Henry's dedication to learning 'amidst all the business of the realm and indeed of the whole world, scarcely a day passes in which you do not devote some portion of your time to reading books, enjoying the society of those philosophers of old'.[6] Erasmus also wrote on educational theory. *Civilitie of Childhood*, the equivalent of a code of conduct for children, was first published in 1532 and went through several editions indicating it was popular and advised children to show deference to all adults irrespective of class. Erasmus and Elyot were not the only ones to write on this subject and there were various books setting out the rules for courtesy as well as simple activities such as dressing, eating and talking.

The demands for study guides increased as the number of students grew. These guides were compiled for both tutors and pupils. One of the guides, *Tenures*, written by Thomas Lyttleton, was first published in the early 1480s which although prior to the Tudors was the first treatise on English Law and was presumably used by those attending the Inns of Court. The treatise focused on Land Law such as freehold rights, tenancy in fee and as expected by the title, tenures. Rights in relation to the land were of utmost importance so this was likely a valuable book to students and the aristocracy, as well as to the development of case law. Demand for books on history also increased as not only could they be used by scholars but also by those seeking to read about the successes of past leaders. History provided a moral compass and was particularly useful for men wishing to learn about war techniques. It also entertained with stories of heroes and battles. Henry VII was clearly interested in preserving the history of England and his dynasty and he invited Polydore Vergil, a renowned humanist scholar from Urbino to England to write its history. The resultant *Anglica Historia* printed in 1534 is an important work amongst those wishing to study history but it should be noted that it is not entirely accurate and might be partial towards its patron. Along with historical accounts of military prowess came manuals on warfare and military techniques. Probably the most surprising of these was *Book of Fayttes of Armes and of Chyvalrye* which on the face of it doesn't sound too surprising but it was actually a translation of *Livre des fais d'armes et de chevalerie* written by Christine de Pisan. It was rare for females to write books but to write one on warfare was totally unheard of. Caxton translated and published the book in 1489 and it is effectively a manual on strategy, gunpowder technology and Just War.

As writing was taught as a completely separate skill to reading and those who could read might wish to learn to write, publications on this subject gradually became available. Books teaching people how to write began to be published towards the end of the fifteenth century. Children and adults could use these to teach themselves and if they persevered to write in different styles. *A Book Containing Divers Sorts of Hands* was published in 1571 and gave instruction in various handwriting styles.

As we have seen in Chapter Eight, religion was extremely important to the Tudors, making books on spirituality prevalent amongst all classes, the Bible being the most important among them. Those who could not afford a Bible had the opportunity to purchase pamphlets, produced cheaply and containing sermons and ballads of a religious theme. At the beginning of the Tudor dynasty, the Bible in use was the Vulgate written in Latin and had been translated from Hebrew and Greek by St Jerome in 382 AD. The name originated from the fact it was written in Latin which was known as the 'vulgar' or common tongue. As English became more widely used in texts scholars began focusing their attention on translations of the Bible. There were also the 'classics' such as the *Fables of Aesop* which would be fashionable to own but it was not enough to merely own the book, conversation in polite circles could often focus on literature making it necessary to be able to refer to a passage or quote within conversation.

There were no female authors of fiction. Even in areas of women's expertise such as embroidery, there were no popular female authors. It was deemed inappropriate for females to express strong opinions in public, so the only publications by females were translations of religious works originally published by others. Books aimed at women increased in the sixteenth century but tended to be based on the skills society deemed useful for them, such as pattern books for sewing, lacemaking, embroidery, music and housekeeping. Books on housekeeping included advice and recipes for using herbs for medicinal purposes indicating that women were responsible for health concerns especially those who might not be able to afford a doctor or tinctures from the apothecaries. As previously discussed, girls learnt from their mother how to use herbs for medicine but those who could afford books could further their knowledge through reading. Recipe books were published consisting of recipes for making ink, soap and different colour dyes for women to use in dress making or for their favours and ribbons.

With the printing press making the creation of books much faster, books were published on a variety of topics including many instructional works dedicated to sports such as hunting, archery, angling, hawking and even astronomical almanacs. Turberville's *Booke of Faulconrie*, published 1575 and second book *The Noble Arte of Venerie or Hunting*, published in 1576 were very popular amongst those fond of hunting and hawking as they discussed the breeding of falcons and how to arrange a hunt, whilst those interested in archery could read books on advice of how to stand and to focus on the target, not the arrow end. The *Boke of St Albans* was printed in 1486 and was compiled of information on hunting, falconry and heraldry. The reader could learn about the differing types of birds, how to care for and train them. The book was reprinted in 1496 by Wynkyn de Worde and this time had the additional *The Treatyse of Fysshynge with an Angle* which discussed fishing, tackle and advised on the different types of fish that could be caught in freshwater. For those interested in hunting, hawking and fishing the second edition of *The Boke of St Albans* would be perfect as it covered all three topics in one book.[7]

There were of course pastimes that did not involve a large amount of action, you only need to visit a historical house with a Tudor Garden to see that they became extremely popular under the Tudors. The wealthy would spend their fortunes on pleasure gardens with their beautiful mazes and knot gardens to enjoy but these also provided sustenance and often included a herb garden, fruit and vegetable plants and trees. Authors began to write on the subject, providing advice on how to create and care for gardens. Whilst the wealthiest would have gardeners to do this for them, those who looked after their own could begin advancing their knowledge and improving their gardens. Thomas Hill's *The Gardener's Labyrinthe* was one such book, published in 1577. Another more relaxing pastime was the game of chess which was also deemed as intellectual and was taught to children. Caxton translated *Liber de Lude Scacchorum* by Jacob de Cessoles into English and published it as *The Game and Playe of the Chesse*. It was in fact only his second book to be published, revealing how popular the game must have been to spend the time translating the work then publishing it.

Books for the purpose of recreational reading increased in availability and popularity. Myths and legends were extremely popular so books such as *Le Morte d'Arthur* and *Bevis of Hampton* featuring stories of chivalry were still printed under the Tudors. The Arthurian stories remained prevalent, hence the name of Henry VII's first son and heir. *History of the Kings of Britain* written in the twelfth century by Geoffrey de Monmouth was still held in great esteem as was the chivalric romance *Sir Gawain and the Green Knight* written in the fourteenth century in verse. Due to the popularity of the legend of King Arthur and his Knights of the Round Table, short stories, often written in verse, began to be published featuring tales of noblemen and romance, always with a happy ending, making recreational reading more affordable and available to a wider audience. Caxton translated *Knight of the Tower* for his own daughters, a book of moral tales which he believed was essential reading for gentlewomen. Another fourteenth-century book that remained popular throughout the Tudor reign was *Mandeville's Tales* which implies it is the account of an English knight and his tale of travelling from England to the Holy Land and Asia. It is unlikely it was written by an Englishman but the book remained popular due its tales of the wonders of Asia, a delight for those who could never envision travelling so far. Books of far-off lands with different animals and cultures were of interest to readers as not many had the ability to travel, *Mandeville's Tales* and Sir Walter Raleigh's *The Discovery of the Large, Rich and Beautiful Empire of Guiana* gave people the opportunity to experience the delights and discoveries of foreign lands. One book we still hear of today is *Utopia*, written by Thomas More. First published in Latin in 1516, it was later translated into English in 1551. Utopia was a fictional island where there was an idealist society established on humanist ideologies. The community in Utopia were tolerant of religion and education was provided to all at no cost. Another that is still in print today is John Foxe's *Acts and Monuments* (Book of Martyrs), a narrative of Protestant martyrs and their treatment including, but not limited to, those condemned by Mary I. It was first published in 1563 under the name *Actes and Monuments of These Latter Perilous Times* and later *The Book of Martyrs: A History of the Persecution of the*

Protestants, and has continued to be printed since. Cathedrals were ordered to have a copy and copies were donated or purchased for parish churches from 1571.

Poetry was also sought after and could be produced in pamphlets as well as books enabling the lower classes to purchase poetry. One of the most famed poets of the era was Thomas Wyatt, he was imprisoned as a possible participant in the Anne Boleyn scandal, but luckily released. None of his poems were published in his own lifetime but under Elizabeth I, *Tottel's Miscellany* was published in 1557 containing ninety-six of Wyatt's poems along with poems by Henry Howard, Earl of Surrey. Wyatt was likely the inspiration for many of the later Tudor poets. *Faerie Queene* by Edmund Spenser had its first three books published around 1589 and was instantly popular for being written in English rather than the traditional Latin used for poetry, but also for being excellent prose.[8] *The Shepherd's Calendar* also by Spenser was printed four times during the reign of Elizabeth after initially being published in 1579. *The Shepherd's Calendar* featured twelve poems, one for each month on topics from romance to religion. Spenser is buried in Westminster Abbey where his funeral was paid for by the Earl of Essex. *Pastime of Pleasure, or the History of Grand Amour and La Bel Pucell*, written by Stephen Hawes, a Groom of the King's Chamber was a popular poem printed by de Worde. The poem encouraged gentlemen to learn and display virtuous behaviour. Another option for the less well-off was to purchase a pamphlet of a ballad. These were widely available, cheap to produce and to purchase and often included attractive woodcut illustrations. Ballad singers could be found throughout London and no doubt other cities singing the ballads whilst selling printed copies.

Many books were dedicated to the reigning monarch or a member of the nobility either as gratitude to the author's patron or with the hope of seeking one. *Atlas* written by Christopher Saxton featured Elizabeth on its cover when it was published in 1579. As the name suggests the book included thirty-four coloured maps of the counties of England and Wales but was the first book to chart the counties leading the way in cartographic studies.

By the end of the Tudor reign, although books were much more widely available, the cost of printing remained high and therefore there were very few books available aimed at children. The options for children remained with nursery rhymes, stories and as they matured, the books written for adults, depending on their literacy. Caxton's printing press had successfully widened the audience of readers and he had largely increased the number of books available in the vernacular. At the time of his death he had published seventy-four titles in English, twenty of these he had completed the translation from the original language himself and had provided readers with a broad range of topics from romance to history. His assistant Wynkyn de Worde continued Caxton's work when he died in 1491 and published books on history, theology, instructional manuals and the ever-popular translations of the classics amongst other subjects. Despite this, books remained a valuable commodity and were usually bequeathed in wills to family and friends or in the case of scholars to educational establishments. Henry VIII received various books from his grandmother Lady Margaret Beaufort upon her death including Froissart's *Chronicles of the Hundred Years' War* in which England defeated France. At the time of his own death, Henry VIII's library at Greenwich, built during his reign, held three hundred and twenty-nine books. Unfortunately, the titles are lost to us. This might not seem like a lot but this is only one library and it is known Henry VIII also took books with him when he travelled between residences.

For adults, it seems that you could buy a book on most topics and if you were wealthy enough could have your own transcribed by hand with beautiful illuminations. The increase in available books written in the vernacular certainly helped to increase literacy among the lower classes who by the end of the period could purchase books and pamphlets on a variety of topics from religion, song, and manners to romance and chronicles. As the number of printing presses increased and literacy spread, more people had the opportunity to self-educate through purchasing and borrowing books or pamphlets although the cost of printed material still remained unaffordable to some. By the end of the Tudor reign, reading material could be bought across the country, pedlars would travel the countryside selling books, pamphlets and broadsheets; the Tudor version of a newspaper. People could purchase material on all subjects including joke and riddle books, educational subjects, encyclopedias and romance from pedlars and even from country fairs whilst in London booksellers set up stalls across the city, especially in St Paul's Churchyard which became a haven for those hoping to increase their literacy skills or enhance their library.

Music and dancing were an integral part of Tudor life and the English were known to be accomplished musicians. All classes were required to have a knowledge of dancing if they wished to partake in social activities. Music and dancing were central to the majority of entertainment and was often the way in which couples met. Music was fundamental to many aspects of Tudor life largely due to the importance of religion but also for entertainment. Music could be found in religious ceremonies, pageants, events such as coronations, births and funerals and for entertainment, both on a large scale and within the privy chamber of the monarch. Musicians were also present to announce the arrival of royalty and those in the royal household might also wear the Tudor livery of green and white.

The types of music and dance differed between the classes. Whilst the wealthy could afford the newest instruments and musicians to entertain them as well as dance masters to instruct them, the lower classes had neither the time to practice nor the resources to purchase expensive instruments, retain a dance master or tutor to teach them. All classes partook in the singing of madrigals, a secular composition with multiple singers, and used music and singing for entertainment and for religious purposes. Singing and the playing of instruments was common in the homes of lower classes, public inns, the great houses of the aristocracy where guests would be expected to join the fun and even on the decks of ships. Sir Francis Drake is known to have had an orchestra aboard the Golden Hind.

Boys could study music at Oxford and Cambridge with the latter being the first to offer a degree in the subject, but the curriculum centered on theory and did not include instruction in playing, although some colleges did provide communal instruments for practice. Students, though, would have to refrain from playing instruments during hours assigned for studying. For those of the lower classes, playing an instrument was often self-taught or by practising with someone of their acquaintance who could play. The alternative was an education provided by the Church through a song school. Boys enrolled at a song school would receive a general education but would also be taught music, making the Church dominant in musical education. The Reformation did cause a decline in the number of boys receiving this type of education but it did not cease entirely.

There were many instruments available consisting of wind, percussion and stringed instruments. Hautboys, sackbuts and bagpipes were the most common instruments amongst the lower classes whilst the wealthy would often own harps, virginals, clavichords, lutes and viols which were played like a bow, similar to a violin. A hautboy is similar to the modern oboe and a sackbut similar to a trombone. A shawm was a flute-like double-reed instrument that had six keys and one for the thumb and was played by all classes and the bombard was a larger version of the shawm. One instrument which sounds similar to that of a violin was the hurdy-gurdy. These are string instruments that have a hand-crank that turns a wheel making a sound against the strings. There are also small keys that when pressed against the strings alter the sound. Instruction manuals were available but the majority of instructional books on music were imported, which meant they were not within reach of the lower classes. Clavichords were a type of stringed keyboard instrument which Margaret and Mary were both accomplished at playing. The lute, owned and played by all of the children of Henry VII, was a stringed instrument where the strings were plucked with nails or with a quill plectrum. Fiddles and rebecs were also common, both similar to one another, played with a bow but the pitch produced by the rebec was higher than that of the fiddle. Many of the percussion instruments are still played today including the triangle. There were also cymbals, rattles, a timbre that was similar to today's tambourine and kettledrums that were suspended from the player's waist.

All of the Tudor monarchs had many musicians at the royal court including minstrels, viol players, trumpeters, and other instrument players. Margaret, Henry and Edward are all known to have had their own company of minstrels even as children. It is no wonder they all loved music as they matured. Minstrels could be musicians who sought to entertain patrons whenever they could in the hopes of further patronisation whilst others were professionals recruited to aristocratic households. Minstrels could sing, play instruments and could often add an element of jesting to their entertainment. Some were extremely physically talented and could entertain with acrobatics, contortionism, tumbling or even performing with animals, making it sound similar to a visit to the circus; these individuals were often employed as jesters. They would often create songs about historic events or use others' work and embellish it. Minstrels sought positions in the royal household and the homes of the nobility and those successful would play appropriate music for each occasion including formal entertainments, in the privy chamber of their host and even during mealtimes. At the royal court, those dining would be entertained either by music from the royal minstrels or the voices of the Chapel Royal. Whilst after dinner it would be the courtiers turn to provide the entertainment by showing their skill on an instrument, singing or reciting poetry. During the reign of Henry VIII *Behold the Sovereign Seed* was a popular choice to sing by the courtiers:

> Behold the soveren sede of this rosis twayn,
> Renewde of God for owre consolacion
> By dropys of grace that on them down doth rays;

Through whose swete showris now sprong ther is ayer
A rose most riall with levis fresh of hew,
All myrthis to maynten, all sorous to subdewe[9]

Music could be performed by professionals as well as courtiers, of which almost all would have been taught to play instruments as a child. The type of instrument played by a professional musician would influence where they played. Instruments such as the virginals and lute tended to be used for private entertainment in the privy chamber whilst instruments producing louder notes such as hautboys would be used in larger gatherings and ceremonies where more people needed to be able to hear the music. This of course meant those playing in the privy chamber often found more favour as they were more likely to be noticed by the nobility or the monarch. Those who attracted the attention of a wealthy patron might find themselves working as a tutor for an aristocratic family or even the royal children as Giles Duwes had done. It was not only the royal court who employed musicians, the wealthy would have musicians in their households who would be expected to entertain guests but they would also have instruments available for guests to play themselves.

Sacred music for religious ceremonies and services became less important following the Reformation but did not diminish entirely. Prior to the Reformation, chapel singers and choirs were vital and also an indication of wealth. Henry VIII was constantly seeking to improve his choir for the Chapel Royal which sometimes meant pinching those from other choirs. One of those who Henry VIII noticed in another's court was Mark Smeaton, the musician of humble origins who was executed for alleged adultery with Anne Boleyn. Smeaton was initially a member of Cardinal Thomas Wolsey's chapel until he obtained a position within Henry VIII's privy chamber. Smeaton was a talented player of the lute, regals and virginals and could also sing and dance. Most sacred music was plainsong but the newly introduced polyphonic music could be heard on occasions at the royal court, homes of the nobility or wealthy religious houses. Polyphonic music included two melodies that were played or sung at the same time to create a completely different sound to the usual plainsong which featured only one melody. Some educational theorists did not approve of polyphonic music in religious services as they felt people might attend church to enjoy the music rather than to pray. To this end, the Prayer Book of 1552 reduced the amount of music in church services but choirs and church music returned under the reign of Mary and was retained by Elizabeth, who although not Catholic, liked music and did not wish for music to be reduced in the services she attended.

The Tudor monarchs were all enthusiastic musicians. Especially Henry VIII who was an accomplished musician, dancer and composer.[10] Henry VIII adored music and was keen to have the very best performers at his court. He brought Dionysius Memo, the organist of St Mark's Cathedral, Venice to court in 1516 and gave him the position of head musician and chaplain, at one point sitting for four hours straight listening to the organist play.[11] In 1540, he had thirty-seven musicians which increased to fifty-eight by 1547.[12] He employed musicians from abroad and had a large collection of his own instruments at the time of his death, including seventy-two flutes and seventy-six recorders, an instrument that is still played today. Henry also owned viols, lutes, harps, flutes, shawns, bagpipes and more. Elizabeth also loved music and in 1575 issued a monopoly of twenty-five years to Thomas Tallis and William Byrd for printing polyphonic music. Tallis was an accomplished composer in English, Latin, French and Italian whilst Byrd was employed at the Chapel Royal. The monopoly was an unusual one at the time but restricted them to music that could be played in church or chamber. The first publication under the monopoly was *Cantiones quae ab argumento sacrae vocantur* featuring sixteen compositions by Tallis and fifteen by Byrd and was dedicated to Elizabeth.[13] If you attend church today you may hear *The Great Service* which was written by Byrd, which indicates just how popular it was to have lasted so many years. Byrd would later go on to compose songs of love and other non-religious topics.

Printed music became more popular in approximately 1550 but even then, as books were still relatively expensive, it was common for the books to be shared so all could play from the same book. The publication of secular music also became more common with lyrics in the vernacular whilst sacred music tended to remain with Latin lyrics. Pricksongs were music made by notation or dots accompanied by words rather than sheet music and books of pricksong became common for both secular and sacred music. A major contribution to printed music was the publication of *The Whole Booke of Psalms* in 1562. This was made up of paraphrased psalms that could be sung, making them effectively hymns. Prior to this, the only singing in church services was done by choirs. The congregation were there to worship and could recite psalms, but they did not sing. This book, an English version of the *Geneva Psalter* was introduced by the Puritans, made the singing of hymns in church possible and continued to play a role in church services throughout the reign of Elizabeth I.

Dance manuals were produced explaining the social role of dancing but also included the steps of particular dances although they did not include the accompanying music. Thomas Elyot in *The Book Named the Governor* upheld the idea that aristocracy should learn to dance and dancing skills were necessary for courtiers. However, it is noted by Castiglione in *The Book of the Courtier* that regardless of how skilled a courtier might be in dance they should remain humble and should not appear as if they have spent much time practising and 'the Courtier ought to have a care, for when dancing in the presence of many and in a place full of people, it seems to me that he should preserve a certain dignity, albeit tempered with a lithe and airy grace of movement'.[14] New dances were sometimes introduced from Europe, and one of these was the stately Pavane, which became one of the most common dances after the summit meeting between Henry VIII and Francis I of France in 1520, known as the Field of the Cloth of Gold. The event lasted over two weeks and was intended to secure friendship between the two kingdoms. It was also a huge entertainment. The introduction of more cosmopolitan dances was largely due to musicians being recruited from across the continent to England by wealthy patrons where their music would influence the dance. Ambassadors, dance masters and ladies-in-waiting who had served abroad could also introduce new dances on their return. In turn, courtiers sought to imitate the royal court and would introduce new music and dances into their own households, servants would do the same and so they would disseminate through the classes. Lower classes would be unable to afford the costly musicians and instruments but they had their own instruments to play with and were more than capable of dancing, less formally than the royal court but I am sure, just as fun.

There were a number of dances at the Tudor court which varied in the number of people who could participate and how energetic they were. The dances chosen would often be selected according to the type of celebration and attendees. As mentioned, the Stately Pavane was a rather formal dance with slow steps that could be danced in groups of three people whilst the Spanish Pavane was more lively and less formal. The Basse was fairly sedate with partners moving through slow gliding steps in a graceful manner, popular during masques and court entertainments but likely not so popular amongst the lower classes, whilst the Tourdion was much more energetic requiring leaping across the floor. Elizabeth I's favourite was the Galliard which she was still impressively dancing in her sixties. The Galliard required the men to lift their partner and perform leaps, making it a very lively dance. Another of the livelier dances was La Volta, men would pick up and spin their female partner, often so fast caution would be needed to ensure gowns remained in place. La Volta was frowned upon as inappropriate for aristocracy by some, but Elizabeth I, never one to be told what she must and must not do, not only allowed it to be danced in her court but danced it herself.

One dance that didn't require partners and was devised for many dancers was the Branles, this was danced by all classes as the steps were very easy to learn and required little skill. Court entertainments would have been observed by servants who would imitate the steps, or as close as possible and so the dances of the lower classes were probably very similar but possibly with less complex steps making them easier to be taught to friends during entertainments.

Drama became ever more popular under the Tudors and was a pastime enjoyed by all classes. Early in the Tudor reign, plays were almost exclusively religious in theme, and could be categorised as miracle, mystery or morality. All three told stories from the scriptures or other religious teachings, morality was the theme whereas miracle and mystery determined who was performing. Morality plays date from the fifteenth century and were based on themes of virtue and the human soul, the performances showing the struggle between good and evil. The most commonly performed included *Noah's Flood* and *The Fall of Lucifer*.[15] When plays were performed by members of a guild they were known as mystery plays as the guild members were members of 'misteries'. Miracle plays were those performed by actors that although they might be professional or amateur, they were not members of any guild. Guilds competed to put on a show of a cycle of mystery plays which were staged in towns around the country, often during religious festivals. These religious-themed plays were typical at the beginning of Henry VII's reign but as reformist ideas began to spread from the continent, these moralising religious tales were gradually eclipsed by the more fashionable secular themes until eventually, William Shakespeare developed the drama of the Middle Ages into the type of play we are familiar with today. Shakespeare, who began his work in theatre around 1585, was not the first to deviate from the traditional morality plays but was immensely successful at incorporating the traditional morality themes along with new Renaissance ideas making himself the most memorable playwright of his time. His first play *The Contention between the Two Noble*

Houses of York and Lancaster was performed in 1592 and by the end of the Tudor reign, twenty-four of his productions would have been performed. Comedies and tragedies, mostly focusing on historical events such as the reign of Richard III, began to emerge under the Tudors with elements of vice and virtue shown through the humour.

All of the Tudor monarchs enjoyed drama. Henry VIII employed four professional actors and their apprentice because he enjoyed the performances so much and bands of travelling players were welcome at the Tudor court but the general public was unfortunately excluded from these events. Educational establishments would also produce plays, sometimes performed by students, sometimes by troupes of actors, based on comedy and the classics with the aim of helping students with their studies in an enjoyable way. This extended to some of the grammar schools where boys might learn drama but this was not a privilege generally afforded to the humbler schools where drama did not form part of the curriculum.

Theatre, though, was not just restricted to the aristocracy, bands of players would travel the country, performing at inns, town squares and villages, though these were not approved of by the government. Stage plays were disapproved of by the government as their subjects were often based on what they considered to be indecent topics or individuals such as Robin Hood. The government felt such plays would cause more people to take the law into their own hands and would result in more crime. As drama became more widespread, the Tudors were determined to control it by requiring each company of actors to be authorised by either a nobleman or justiciars and plays were to be licensed by the Lord Chamberlain. The first permanent stage was erected at the Red Lion in Whitechapel in 1567 but it was not until 1576 that the first theatre was built in Shoreditch and was named very simply, The Theatre. Due to the disapproval of the Mayor of London, many theatres were built outside the City of London. The Amphitheatre held over two thousand spectators and was largely open-roofed but the more expensive seats and the stage were covered over. The Hall was smaller, holding only one thousand but was completely covered meaning entry was expensive. There was also the Globe, a round wooden structure at which Shakespeare was both a player and a shareholder and a replica of the theatre remains open to this day. The programme at theatres changed quite often meaning people could visit frequently and see a different play each time with trumpets announcing the beginning of the afternoon's entertainment. Other entertainers would also perform at theatre productions to entertain observers between acts. Tumblers, dancers, clowns and even fireworks might make an appearance at one of the theatres, the fireworks entertaining a much bigger audience than just those inside the theatre. Although the majority of plays were based on religious themes and took place largely at times of Christian festivals they were not limited to these times. Individual plays could be performed wherever there might be an audience but larger events such as festivals would include a series of individual plays known as pageants which would be performed in sequence forming a longer play with a particular theme. These larger entertainments could be performed from wagons that were pulled through the streets so spectators could see each pageant as it passed.

Mumming was another form of drama, popular during the major holidays such as Christmas. Mummers plays were performed by amateurs and the plot usually featured a champion who would be killed in a sword fight then brought back to life. One extremely popular theme was St George and the Dragon. The performers would be masked or their faces disguised in some way. Masques, first recorded at the royal court under the reign of Henry VIII in 1512, became very popular, especially in the Elizabethan era. Masques consisted of music, singing, dancing and acting and were themed. Those featuring ancient gods and goddesses were a common feature at Elizabeth's court and became more popular than tournaments which might indicate Elizabeth preferred the spectacle and excitement of a masque to watching men fight and joust. Elizabeth was extremely fond of summer progresses when she would spend time travelling around the country, staying with nobility and enjoying their hospitality and entertainment. Those whom Elizabeth stayed with would often organise a masque for her enjoyment and dependent on the length of her stay would also arrange other entertainments including actors' troupes, hunting and hawking.

'Fools' were a common feature in the homes of the aristocracy and the royal court. Henry VIII had a fool named John Goor when he was aged ten but the most famous of his fools was Will Somers. Most fools during the Tudor era were people with a learning disability and Somers was no different, and he had a carer assigned to him. Fools, especially Somers, played a prominent role in entertainments at court and could jest and make fun of royalty and nobility in ways that no other person would be allowed.[16] Others included Diego the Spanish Fool who would wear a saddle and race around the court like a horse. The court would be entertained by individuals who would do bizarre acts such as eating coals. The Tudor children probably had immense fun with all the music, drama and entertainment available at the royal households.

Books, music and drama were a large part of both religion and entertainment under the Tudors for all classes but there were also many other pastimes the Tudors enjoyed.

Chapter Nine

Pastimes for All

As we have seen, education during the Tudor era was hard work with formal education often consisting of a six-day week. For those who received their education through on-the-job learning, there was little time for pastimes. Those with the privilege of private tutors, although they still studied hard, had a little more time for pastimes. For those in employment, their week also consisted of six days with usually very long working hours and only Sundays and holy days free. Sunday was seen as the day of rest where the population would attend religious services and spend the day with family and friends. Many of the pastimes the Tudors enjoyed are still popular today, although some might have changed whilst others are certainly no longer in existence.

As with education, pastimes differed between the social classes but there are pastimes that many of varying classes partook in. During the sixteenth century, it was deemed necessary for all men to be ready for war. For this reason, pastimes with a martial overtone were very popular and encouraged by the monarchy and government to the point that in 1512 Henry VIII banned certain pastimes except at Christmastime in an attempt to maintain the practice of archery but to also ensure the common people were fit to work.[1] At Christmas, games such as skittles, quoits, cards, dice and tennis could be played under supervision of their betters but this did not mean they were not played throughout the year along with the gambling that took place within the games. For the aristocracy some pastimes were seen to be beneficial to their education as Ascham declares:

> to ride cumlie: to run faire at the tilte or ring: to plaie at
> all weapons: to shote faire in bow, or surelie in gon: to

vaut lustily: tu runne: to leape: to wrestle: to swimme: To daunce cumlie: to sing, and playe of instruments cunningly: to Hawke: to hunte: to playe at tennes, & all pastimes generally, which be ioyned with labor, vsed in open place, and on the day light, conteining either some fitte exercise for warre, or some pleasant pastime for peace, be not onelie cumlie and decent, but also verie necessarie, for a Courtlie Ientleman to vse[2]

Tournaments were possibly the most exciting pastime, particularly with the upper classes and like hunting provided a means for men to train for battle, exercise, as well as show off their skills to spectators, usually with the opportunity to win a valuable prize which was often awarded by a noble or royal female. In medieval times, tournaments took on the form of a full mock battle but by the Tudor era, this had become more of a display of skill and pageantry. By this time tournaments were far more controlled events, with fewer competing at a time and were planned diligently with music and other entertainment throughout. Tournaments could include mounted combat or on-foot fighting, usually fought using sword, spear and mace; the sword, of course being blunted to decrease the risk of injury, although it still remained a dangerous pastime. Mêlées were no longer as common as in previous years but still took place on occasion. The mêlée was usually two teams who would face each other in combat with one team winning but as they were a free-for-all, could prove to be dangerous as weapons clashed around the participants. The tourney was usually followed by the joust, the most popular attraction of the tournament. Two opponents would face each other on opposite sides of a barrier before racing towards each other on horseback with a lance. The aim of the joust was to unhorse an opponent using a lance and allowed participants to practice their skills for war as well as providing spectators with the opportunity to view the most exquisite pageantry as competitors would sometimes arrive in themed costumes. If an opponent wasn't unhorsed, the winner was determined by points scored for the breaking of lances and hits to the helm. Tournaments usually revolved around a theme beginning with a challenge such as the tournament held at Westminster in 1511 by Henry VIII to celebrate the birth of a boy. The theme for the tournament was four knights, Coeur Loyal (Henry), Vaillant Desyr (Sir Thomas Knyvet), Bon Vouloir (Sir William Courtenay) and Joyeux Penser (Sir Edward Neville) had been sent to England by the Queen of Noble Heart to challenge all comers to celebrate the birth of a boy. Once the challenge was issued courtiers could sign up to participate as an answerer. A procession usually began the tournament, followed by the joust and dancing and pageantry would also be incorporated into the celebrations.

Henry VIII was the only Tudor monarch to participate in tournaments, Mary I and Elizabeth I were unable to do so as females whilst Henry VII preferred to watch, and Edward VI was too young to participate. Henry VIII was a very accomplished jouster, participating in disguise in the first joust since his coronation, he also reached the highest score in the 1511 tournament and often partook in jousts and tournaments, with his courtiers, especially Charles Brandon, Duke of Suffolk, who became his brother-in-law when Brandon married Henry VIII's sister, Mary. Only the upper classes participated, however attendance was open to wider classes and provided the opportunity to observe the elaborate costumes and sportsmanship, although they did have to pay for admittance. Once admitted they would also have the opportunity to watch puppet shows and other entertainments in-between the main events. The joust could also be extremely dangerous and could result in death, injuries included the loss of Sir Francis Bryan's eye and Henry VIII's injury to his leg which would result in a wound causing pain for the remainder of his life. Riding at the ring would also feature at tournaments which was much safer than jousting but required the same skill and marksmanship. A ring would be suspended on a thread and the rider would be required to put their lance through the centre, breaking the thread as they galloped past so the ring remained on the lance. Tournaments were often a feature of large celebrations such as weddings or religious celebrations.

Other martial sports included wrestling and running at the quintain which was practice for the joust as the participant had to hit a target rather than a competitor. Wrestling could be practiced from childhood; it was a very common sport across all classes and was another opportunity to place bets on the outcome. Henry VIII lost a wrestling match to Francis I of France during the Field of the Cloth of Gold. Running at the quintain provided youths with the opportunity to practice before attempting to participate in riding at the ring or a full joust. The rider would attempt to hit the target which pivoted so they had to be swift to avoid it swinging around and hitting them in the back as they passed. Adults would practice at the tiltyard. For the more adventurous, they could attempt to hit targets in the water whilst sailing on the Thames. This version was likely more popular with children and youths whose families were required to take a boat across the river frequently. One of the more violent martial sports was cudgel play which due to its limited requirements in equipment and violence was likely played by the lower classes. The game involved two opponents who each held a stick and the aim was to be the first to draw blood from your opponent, a much more dangerous alternative to the practice of sword-fighting with wooden swords and likely faced much disapproval from the royal court.

For royalty and the aristocracy, hunting was the most favourable pastime but also provided the opportunity to prepare for war. Henry VIII is known to have been a keen hunter and often spent whole days hunting and tiring multiple horses.[3] The most common quarry for the aristocracy was the deer, also known as a hart to the Tudors, lower classes would instead hunt fox and other smaller animals. Royalty and many of the aristocracy, particularly the nobility kept specific dogs and horses just for use in hunting but it was not always conducted from horseback, some would wait on a platform whilst the animals were flushed towards them. Lower classes were limited in their hunting as it was a crime to hunt in a royal forest, punishable by death if poachers were discovered at night. They also lacked horse and hound to participate in the same manner as the wealthy.[4] Most would use a longbow for hunting, although others preferred the crossbow. Hunting was a pastime that required knowledge including which hounds are best suited for specific prey, the terminology of the hunt and identifying prize catches and therefore, books were published on the subject. Sir Thomas Elyot advised that hunting 'increaseth in them both agility and quickness, also sleight and policy to find such passages and straits, where they might prevent or entrap their enemies. Also by continuance therein they shall easily sustain travailing wars, hunger and thirst, cold and heat'.[5] Hunting was effectively target practice on moving targets so had the educational aspect of preparing men for battle if required. Women could also join the hunt, Margaret is known to have killed a deer on her way to her marriage in Scotland and Henry VII was joined by his daughter Mary along with Katharine of Aragon to hunt in the royal deer parks. The kills from a hunt would provide sustenance for the household and were also often sent as gifts to others.

Hawking was another form of hunting, often enjoyed in winter when harts were less visible for hunting, of which the wealthy aristocracy and royalty were keen and provided a more apt pastime for gentlewomen. Hawking was a costly pastime so participation was limited to the wealthy, even some of the aristocracy could not afford to participate unless they were lucky enough to be invited by another and were able to borrow a bird. The birds were very expensive to purchase as they were a status symbol so the falcon you owned was determined by your rank. The female falcons were preferred as they were larger and kings were able to hunt with Gyrfalcons. The nobility could use species of Peregrines, ladies would use Merlin's, a small species suitable for hunting smaller prey, whilst the lower classes could use Goshawks or Sparrowhawks. It was against the law to own a falcon above your station and according to *The Boke of St Albans*, the punishment was to have your hands cut off. They also required a falconer to train and care for the birds making it an expensive and lengthy pastime. As with hunting, hawking could be done on foot or from horseback and there were different types of hawking, the birds could be trained to catch prey on the ground or from the air. Fishing was also a well-liked pastime with Henry VII rewarding one of Arthur's men for bringing him two fish which were likely caught by Arthur himself at the age of six. Henry VIII and Edward also both enjoyed the sport which appears to have been popular with all classes based on the fact books were published on the subject.[6]

For those not fortunate enough to partake in hunting, they were still encouraged to choose pastimes that would ready them for war and the defence of the kingdom, the main sport being archery using the longbow. The longbow was favoured over the crossbow as the latter was useless in wet weather, a feature we are most used to in England and took longer to reload which could prove deadly in times of war. This did not stop men from purchasing and practising with them which was not favourable with Henry VII or parliament, who declared in 1503, that other than lords, only landowners with rental incomes over a specific amount could shoot a crossbow. Due to the decrease of interest in archery, Henry VIII issued the 'Act concerning the shooting in Longe Bowes'. The Act aimed to increase the practice of archery once again by ensuring all towns provided butts for practice as had been the case in history when archers were a major contributing aspect of the English army and were renowned for their skill in battle. The Act also stated that fathers and masters were tasked with providing a bow and two arrows for boys from the age of seven to seventeen to learn to shoot, those over eighteen were to ensure they had their own bow and four arrows in their home. Henry VIII also ordered that those over the age of twenty-four should not be using butts with a distance of less than 220 yards. This really illustrates how skilled archers were and had incredible strength. In 1512, archery was still showing signs of decline, despite Henry VIII practicing regularly himself and holding competitions at court. It was thought this was due to men playing other sports including bowls, quoits and tennis, To remedy this, action was to be taken against the owners of any premises which allowed these other sports to be played. The Tudor monarchs also tried to regulate the price of bows to ensure even the poor could afford a bow and required bowmakers to have cheap and inexpensive bows for this purpose. Roger Ascham attempted to revitalise the sport with his publication of *Toxophilus* (Lover of the Bow), a book written in English, based on the subject of archery including techniques. However, with the introduction of firearms, archery doesn't appear to have revived, although men still spent Sundays with friends at the butts, which were likely present in all towns and of course they could visit the taverns after practice to drink with friends.

Tennis was popular among all classes although due to differing resources was played differently. Upper classes could play on a tennis court with rackets and lower classes could play anywhere space afforded using the palm of their hands, often known as Balloon Ball or Fives. Lower classes would also create rings on the ground and compete to hit the ball through the rings using a stick or bat if they had one. This game sounds very similar to croquet but was known as Closh. Henry VII was a fan of tennis and built tennis courts at several royal palaces meaning Henry VIII grew up with the opportunity to use them when he visited these palaces. Henry VIII built several more tennis courts at Hampton Court, Whitehall, and St James's Palace and was a keen tennis player as we know from comments made by the Venetian ambassador 'It is the prettiest thing in the world to see him play, his fair skin glowing through a shirt of the finest texture'.[7] Tennis was a spectator sport but the games taking place within royal palaces were only open to courtiers. It provided the opportunity for another very common pastime, gambling. Gambling took place amongst all classes, even royalty, against a variety of sports including jousting, tennis, cards, dice and bowling. Bowling appears to have been a predominantly but not exclusively, upper-class sport of both females and males, with indoor and garden bowling alleys becoming a feature of wealthy homes. Bowling alleys could also be found at the colleges of the university and was seen as a suitable pastime for scholars when not studying. Ecclesiastical men were also not averse to a game of bowls. Lower classes could make their way to one of the many purpose-built alleys in towns or even alehouses to play, due to its increased popularity. For those with few resources, they could make their own 'jacks' and use any type of ball to bowl with. Quoits was another game requiring very little equipment. It was a throwing game that sometimes had a target but this was not required. The quoit could be a stone or a horseshoe. Children could also practice by throwing stones at either a target or by competing for distance, a sling shot would add an extra element of skill to the game and could be made fairly cheaply.

Football was also popular but not quite as we now know it. It was deemed inappropriate for those of the wealthy classes as it often resulted in violence between players and was denounced by those writing at the time about pastimes suitable for aristocracy, having previously been banned in 1314 by Edward II. Essentially the only feature it had in common with today's game is there were goals although at the time these could be miles apart, and two teams. There were no fixed numbers to a team, no other rules, and the off-side rule definitely didn't exist. Matches often occurred between rival villages, all males would join in as well as the occasional female, and did not have a time limit. Players could kick, throw and carry the ball and often resorted to violence to prevent the opposition gaining control of the ball. You could trip, kick and punch the opposition, the game could even result in death due to injuries received during the match. Not all were against the sport, Richard Mulcaster, headmaster of St Paul's thought it was good for building strength but did think it needed rules applying. Henry VIII was also not opposed to the game, he owned football boots and apparently enjoyed playing occasionally even when it was deemed unfitting, although it is doubtful anyone playing with the king intended any violence towards him.[8] It was eventually banned again in 1540, but thankfully for football fans today, the ban did not last long. Football was played throughout the period by the lower classes despite the threat of fines and even imprisonment for playing. Those in the countryside were less at risk of punishment and therefore it was a popular pastime during holidays and Sundays, after attendance at church of course.

There were of course more gruesome pastimes with public executions being a spectator sport. Huge crowds would gather to watch the spectacle of a condemned person making their last speech before being hanged or in other circumstances hanged, drawn and quartered. The aim was to discourage crime and show the consequences of doing so but many attended for the entertainment watching the event and spending the day with friends. Animal sports were also popular including bull-baiting, bear-baiting and cock-fighting. Bear and bull-baiting often took place in purpose-built pits. Bear-baiting consisted of a bear being tethered and dogs being released to fight the animal. All classes could attend and Henry VIII is believed to have arranged events at court for himself and courtiers. Wagers could be placed on how many dogs would survive.

As bears had to be imported, bull-baiting was more common as the animals were more readily available than bears. It followed the same process where a bull was tethered and trained bulldogs set upon the animal. Various wagers were placed, including by the owners of the dogs, with the prize being awarded to the owner of the dog who was first to bite the animal's snout. Cock-fighting was cheap entertainment but popular amongst all classes. Henry VIII even had cockpits built. The sport saw cockerels fighting each other with wagers being placed on the cocks whilst threshing the cock involved a cockerel or hen being tied or partially buried and spectators would throw stones at the animal. The prize was the animal itself and was awarded to the person who eventually killed it. Even the schools allowed this pastime and would permit the boys to bring their own cocks to school once per year on Shrove Tuesday for cock-fighting. Nowadays these seem very gruesome and cruel but to those in the Tudor era, it was s form of entertainment and the possibility of winning a bird for dinner.

Not all animals were for sport, the Tudors were pet owners just as many are today although cats were definitely not as popular as they are now and prior to the Tudors were thought to be demons. At the royal court, dogs were required to be kenneled except those granted permission by the monarch. Or those belonging to the upper-class ladies who often owned lapdogs. Many ladies doted on their dogs and spend many hours training and playing with them. Marmosets were popular amongst the wealthy including Katharine of Aragon, and birds were kept by many. Popinjays were generally the most expensive due to them having to be imported but were bright with beautiful colours and could be taught to speak. Dangerous in the Tudor court if they repeat what they hear! Nightingales and larks were far more affordable and were kept in cages as songbirds. Henry VIII owned a pet ferret which was probably the least unusual of his collection of animals, considering he owned the royal menagerie at the Tower of London.

The majority of these entertainments are outdoor pastimes, with the exception of some which could be played indoors by those fortunate to have indoor tennis courts or bowling alleys so during the colder months indoor pastimes became more prevalent. Regardless of class, some winter games were enjoyed by all including skating when the Thames and other rivers froze over. Skates could be made from bones and strapped to the feet making it an inexpensive pastime for all. In the warmer months, the rivers provided the opportunity for swimming but as the first treatise on swimming by Everard Digby wasn't published until 1587 it is unclear how popular swimming was.[9] Football also continued in the winter months but when played on the ice was known as ice camping. All classes would dance and sing as seen in the previous chapter but there were also games involving cards, dice, tables (backgammon) and chess which were played all year.

Chess was primarily played by the wealthy as the board and pieces were expensive but the lower classes did play, they just did not have the same extravagant pieces and boards as the wealthy did. Henry VIII and his court certainly played chess as did Elizabeth and Edward, the latter of which had a chess set from a young age.[10] The game also became very popular amongst the clergy. Chess is a game of skill that had been played for centuries and became an aspect of aristocratic education. The rules changed towards the sixteenth century making it the game we know today. The new rules made it possible for pawns to move two spaces on their first move and castles were introduced. Cards along with dice were popular across all classes as was the opportunity for gambling whether in taverns or stately homes and palaces. Card games included Primero, the aim being to collect a group of cards or one of each suit, bets could be placed at the beginning and during the game as cards were picked and discarded. Another card game that was popular, especially during the reign of Henry VIII, was Pope Joan which required a board or places marked out if a board wasn't available, making it possible for all classes to play. The combinations were named king, queen, jack, pope, game, matrimony and intrigue and were played with fifty-one cards, the eight of diamonds being removed as a 'stop' card. The aim was to dispose of your cards first by laying them in order a little like today's Rummy. The Tudors left a lasting legacy in playing cards too as legend states the Queen is a representation of Elizabeth of York.

There were numerous dice games, some games aimed to reach the score of thirty-one or one hundred by multiple rolls of the dice and was a common game amongst courtiers for gambling including Henry VIII and Mary. Passage was also an option and involved the player rolling three dice until they roll a double. If the double was less than ten, they were out of the game. More than ten, they win and ten exactly, it passes to the next player. Raffles used three dice and the aim was to get all three showing the same number.

Whilst the Tudors might not have had board games like Monopoly and Cluedo they certainly had their own versions. The Philosopher's Game used a double chessboard and Three Men's Morris or Merrels, similar to today's noughts and crosses, were also popular, with the aim being to get three in a row but using a board and pieces. If you achieved a row, you could remove a piece from your opponent. Nine Men's Morris was an expanded version where the winner was the first to remove seven of their opponents' pieces. Goose resembled Snakes and Ladders; the aim was to reach the goose and avoid the places which would send you backwards. Today's Backgammon was the Tudors Tables, a game where the players aimed to clear their opponents' counters by using dice to move their own counters. Shovelboard was common amongst the wealthy classes and was yet another game in which bets could be placed. The players would slide metal pieces down a board or table with the aim of either getting as close to a mark or as far as possible without falling off the edge. Along with chess, one game that is still played today is dominoes, and you guessed it, the Tudors also gambled on dominoes! Henry VIII lost £450 in January 1530 playing the game, a huge sum of money at the time.[11]

Riddles and poetry provided entertainment amongst the classes as well as dancing, music and singing as seen in the previous chapter. Many courtiers tried their hand at poetry including Henry VIII himself but probably the most renowned were Thomas Wyatt, who wrote a poem about the execution of Anne Boleyn, and Philip Sidney, noted for writing the first sequence of sonnets in English. Courtly love was an elegant game played at the royal court involving poetry and the exchange of protestations of love and tokens. Courtiers would play the game but it did not mean there was any genuine affection and it had rules just like any other game as well as a code which courtiers would abide by. The aim was to produce the most intellectual and witty prose or writing to honour the figure of their admiration, sometimes a fictitious person. Courtiers, if they played this game successfully, could find favour and patronage from their social betters but it could also have disastrous consequences if the game went too far.

Women would often embroider in leisure time, having learnt from a young age using a sampler to practice different stitches. Whilst oftentimes there would be a purpose for their needlework or embroidery such as creating something specific, there was also time when ladies would embroider solely for their enjoyment. It was something that could be done in or out of doors and those who could obtain books on embroidery and needlework could develop their skills to create beautiful pieces, including detailed patterns on a gown, sleeves, shirts for their husband and even altar cloths for churches. Working with lace was popular amongst the higher classes. Whilst those of the lower classes might not possess books of intricate embroidery patterns, they would still spend time mending clothes or adding embroidered patterns and detail to clothing if resources permitted.

Drinking establishments provided a venue for amusements such as cards and dice as well as the expected social aspect of drinking. These establishments varied in their class of clientele. Alehouses were often impermanent and provided food and ale or beer to the lower classes. Their trade was high but they were frowned upon as places where men would spend their wages on ale and gambling, leaving little to provide for their family. Taverns generally served more of the well-to-do whilst Inns were prevalent amongst gentlemen and merchants and were permanent fixtures often with boarding for those requiring it. People would also participate in communal drinking which aimed to raise funds for local people in need, whilst churchales were to raise funds for parish expenses.

Yearly entertainments often centered around the Church which remained the heart of festivals and religious celebrations. These events were mostly linked to the liturgical year and whilst they were not standard in England, there were various celebrations that occurred on a large scale across the country. Many parishes had their own way of celebrating festivals and marking important days. The Reformation did affect many of these observances but those changes will not be discussed in any detail. Holy days and seasonal celebrations were enjoyed by all, irrespective of class, they were a time for all to forget about work and enjoy themselves with friends and family.

Christmas as we know it was very different for the Tudors but was still a large celebration. Whereas now we may celebrate with friends and family on Christmas Eve, for the Tudors this was a strict fast day where meat, eggs and cheese were forbidden.[12] Only on Christmas Day could the celebrations really begin and it started with the celebration of three Masses. The twelve days of Christmas were not all celebrated to a huge extent and largely kept to the main days which were Christmas Day, New Year's Day and Twelfth Night. It should be noted that for the Tudors the new year actually began on 25 March which was the Feast of Annunciation. New Year's Day taking place on 1 January was still celebrated as part of the twelve days of Christmas as it had been previously in the Roman age. Christmas Day was not the time for gift exchange as it is now in England and instead this happened on New Year's Day especially in wealthy households. Those of the upper classes would often exchange gifts and this included gifts to their household and servants. For royalty, these gifts could vary from humble to extravagant and there was an expectation of receiving a gift in return. Christmas celebrations in the royal and wealthy households or institutions such as the universities were often presided over by the Lord of Misrule, even the monarch had to abide by their 'rule' during the festivities. For the lower classes celebrating within the community, the Boy Bishop was a popular custom whereby a boy from the church choir would be chosen to lead a procession on certain days during the Christmas celebrations. Wassailing was certainly a practice in which all classes partook. As to whether the extent of fun was the same, we do not know but it is likely the lower classes made much more fun of the tradition. Wassailing involved communal drinking from the same vessel followed by singing. The Christmas festivities ended on

Twelfth Night or Epiphany when following Mass, the entertainment began. For upper classes, this would involve singing and dancing and possibly masques especially in the royal household and the lower classes would also celebrate with singing and dancing. For those lucky enough to have a generous lord with a manor nearby, they might be invited to celebrate the Christmas festivities at the manor including food, drink and entertainment.

Candlemas was the first important event of the year taking place on 2 February. This was seen as the beginning of spring but also the supposed purification of the Virgin Mary. For the church service, all parishioners would attend church and be presented with a candle lit by the parish priest and then join the procession. Not all the Tudor monarchs kept the elaborate services but it is a notable one to mention as at times when it was not banned, whole communities would participate. Next came Lent and Holy Week which was the most extravagant of all the occasions. Shrovetide marked the beginning of Lent and was seen as the last opportunity for fun. It was celebrated with various entertainments including plays, music, dancing and within the royal household, masques. Holy Week began on Palm Sunday with a procession and on Maundy Thursday, most people would attend confession and the churches would be prepared for the Easter celebrations. Good Friday celebrations mainly involved the clergy and laity in the Ceremony of the Creeping Cross where they would crawl to the altar to kiss the feet of the figure of Jesus. They would also make the preparations for Easter Sepulchre on Easter Sunday. This was marked by all candles being extinguished and relit by the priest. Mass was attended by all and once it had ended the celebrations could begin. Celebrations would involve singing, dancing and more flamboyant entertainments at the royal court. Not all of these survived the Reformation and the services that did survive were usually less extravagant. Whitsun was the next event to fall on the liturgical calendar, falling approximately five weeks after Easter. Whitsun was celebrated with games and the selling of church ales which helped to raise funds for the parish. Processions, pageants and plays based on biblical topics were common features of Whitsun celebrations with all welcome to join. Church ales were not restricted to Whitsun and were used throughout the year for fundraising but were a popular part of the Whitsun celebrations.

Corpus Christi fell after Whitsun almost eight weeks after Easter. The festival aimed to remind people of the Eucharist and for this reason did not survive the Reformation but whilst it did exist was a largely popular festival of pageants where villages would compete with other often expanding on the number of plays each year. Processions involved the clergy and members of the council and guild members. In larger towns and cities these processions brought large crowds lining the streets to see the pageants as they passed on carts. One of the most popular plays was a morality play which reminded spectators that they would be judged after death for their deeds.

The wakes occurred at the end of summer and were celebrations of the dedication of the parish churches. Initially these were not set dates but Henry VIII decreed all to be celebrated on the first Sunday of October.[13] The wakes were generally community celebrations relating to their local parish church. Autumn brought the festival of Hallowtide, the feast of the dead. Christians believed this festival would help souls in purgatory. The churches would be lit by candles through the night and the bells would ring accompanied by various entertainments such as music and pageants. Hallowtide did not survive the Reformation due to its belief in purgatory. Other festivals, that there is evidence of, are not part of the liturgical calendar but still provided entertainment for the population whether nationally or locally. Valentine's Day was celebrated with a 'Valentine' being chosen from a group of friends or within the household, although it is not known if this was celebrated nationally or amongst all classes. Tokens were exchanged and those who received a token from their master were usually the luckiest as they would likely receive the most expensive gift. For a servant, this could be something very valuable.

One festival which does not appear to have been celebrated nationally but only in a number of towns and villages was St George's Day on 23 April. Those that did celebrate this day did so by pageants and processions often including models of St George and dragons.

As the weather grew warmer more outdoor celebrations could occur and May Day was celebrated nationally to welcome the summer. Those who participated in May Day festivals often wore garlands and would enter the woods collecting greenery which was known as making the May. As you might expect a maypole was part of the festival and although it was danced around, it did not have the ribbons we associate with maypoles today and instead was decorated with the greenery gathered. The May Day festival allowed further entertainment although slightly mischievous in that stealing a neighbouring village's maypole became a popular part of the celebrations.[14]

Midsummer was important to the Tudors as it marked the summer solstice and as it indicates was the middle of summer which began on May Day and ended with the first harvest in August. It was also the day of the feast of St. John the Baptist on 24 June but the celebrations were rarely linked to this. Bonfires would light up the sky across the country, from the royal court to the countryside, the fire representing the sun, and communities would gather to dance around the fires and celebrate. A cartwheel with hay known as a fiery wheel was often set alight and rolled down a hill, if it reached the bottom still aflame it was believed to indicate a good harvest for the village or town. It was also a time for quarrels to be resolved and the giving of alms to the poor by the wealthier classes. Some areas would have 'Marching Watches' which consisted of parades through the streets with torches accompanied by large colourful model giants and hobby horses. The marching watches also included pageants and Morris dancers providing a wealth of fun, music and drama for spectators. Although many of the elaborate religious festivals did not survive the Reformation, the Church remained central to community entertainments especially to the lower classes who did not have the room to host events or the resources to provide refreshments on a large scale which in turn could benefit the churches through the aforementioned church ales which gave them the opportunity to provide entertainment whilst also fundraising.

For children, many of the basic entertainments haven't changed even today. They still played with toys, they had dolls, drums, hobby horses and even popguns that shot clay pellets. A large number of children's pastimes were easier versions of adult pastimes such as bowling. The children would use marbles instead or a miniature bowls set if it could be afforded. Shuttlecock was played by children using a cork with feathers attached. Wealthy children might have had rackets whilst poorer children would use their hands to play. Today we would use a badminton court to play with a shuttlecock but badminton did not exist so there were no badminton courts available. Instead, shuttlecock was played in any open area unless they were lucky enough to have access to a tennis court they could play in. Many games played by children today were also played by Tudor children; hide and seek, tag and follow the leader. As noted in the previous chapter, aristocratic households often employed minstrels who could provide an alternative entertainment so those children who played at acrobatics and walking on stilts might find themselves recruited when they grew up, provided they were noticed.

Tudor children spent most of their childhood imitating adults. This included being dressed as miniature adults, learning courtesy from a young age and copying ceremonies and rituals for fun. Boys would play at being knights in a game called Sword and Buckler, using wooden swords and shields and pretending to go off to battle to defend their country. They could even play with small toy canons that used real lead powder and as they got older bows and arrows. For the aristocracy, this would be the beginning of their military training. Girls might pretend to be princesses or queens or imitate their mother using a doll to learn how to dress and behave.

Other than animal sports, most of the pastimes are still around today, although some have vastly improved. It is difficult to imagine a football match taking place today with no rules and no limit on the number of players. No wonder it was frowned upon by some. Under the Tudors, the majority worked hard but made up for it on holy days and festivals and regardless of class, the Tudors were definitely gamblers, taking the opportunity to bet on anything and everything. It is apparent the Renaissance affected the Tudors in education but the printing press and the changes to drama through the spread and incorporation of its ideas ultimately led to increased literacy amongst the population as well as impacting education through providing a larger availability of publications for common people as well as schoolmasters and pupils. It also made self-education much more possible than ever before as, once someone was literate, they could expand their learning from religious texts to educational topics, instructional manuals on courtesy and advice books on pastimes. Whilst the Reformation might have impacted on the number of elementary establishments, it is apparent the Tudor monarchs took education seriously. Many benefited from the increase in access to education but that did not stop them from enjoying themselves with various pastimes.

Many aspects of daily life from morning prayers, school and pastimes all had an educational influence on the Tudors and many influential humanists left a legacy still visible today.

Bibliography

Abbreviations

LPFD – Letters & Papers Foreign and Domestic in the reign of Henry VIII.
CSPV – Calendar of State Papers, Venetian
CSPS – Calendar of State Papers, Spain
ELR – Edward VI, Literary Remains
PPE – Privy Purse Expenses

Primary Sources – The National Archives

SP1: *State Papers Henry VIII*
SP10: *State Papers Edward VI*
E36: *Treasury of Receipts, Miscellaneous Books*
E101: *Exchequer, King's Remembrancer, Various Accounts*
LC2: *Lord Chamberlain's Office, Robes and Special Events*

Printed Primary Sources

André, B, *The Life of Henry VIII*, translated by Hobbins, D, (Translation of *Historia regis Henrici Septimi, by Bernard Andreas; edited by James Gairdner; published by Longman, Brown, Green, Longmans and Robert, 1858)*, (Italica Press, New York, 2011)

Ascham, R, *English Works*, edited by Wright, W.A., (Cambridge University Press, London, 1970)

Castiglione, B, *The Book of the Courtier*, translated by Opdycke, L.E. (Dover Publications, 2003)

Colet, J. Dean, *Statutes of Dean Colet: Founder of St. Paul's School... also, A copy of the will of Sir T. Gresham...dated...1575...added, the names of a few eminent persons who were educated at St. Paul's School*, J. Hatchard and J. Richardson, London, (1816)

Edward VI, *Literary remains of King Edward the sixth, edited from his autograph manuscripts with historical notes and a biographical memoir*, ed. J. G. Nicols, 2 vols, London, (1857)

Edward VI, *The Journal of King Edward's Reign*, (Clarendon Historical Society, 1884)

Erasmus, D, *The Education of a Christian Prince*, edited by Jardine, L, (Cambridge University Press, 1997)

Hall, E, *Hall's Chronicle; containing the history of England, during the reign of Henry the fourth, and the succeeding monarchs, to the end of the reign of Henry the Eighth, in which are particularly described the manners and customs of those periods*, (London, 1809)

Hoole, C & Thiselton, M, *A New Discovery of the Old Art of Teaching School*, (copied from a manuscript in the British Library, London, 1660, reprint 1912)

Letters and Papers, Foreign and Domestic, of the reign of Henry VIII, ed. J.S. Brewer, J. Gairdner and R.H. Brodie, 21 vols in 32 parts, and Addenda (London, 1862-1932)

Privy Purse Expenses of the Princess Mary, ed. F. Madden, (London, 1831)

Privy Purse Expenses of Elizabeth of York: Wardrobe Accounts of Edward the Fourth: With a Memoir of Elizabeth of York, and Notes, ed. N.H. Nicolas, (London, 1830)

Records of the Honourable Society of Lincoln's Inn: Black Books, Volume 1, (1422-1586)

The Chronicle and Political Papers of King Edward VI, ed. W.K. Jordan, (George Allen and Unwin Ltd, London, 1966)

The Lisle Letters, ed. St. Clare Byrne, (Penguin, London, 1985)

Vives, J.L, *Tudor School-boy Life: The Dialogues of Juan Luis Vives, Transl. For the First Time into Engli. Together with an Introd. By Watson, F*, (J.M. Dent & Co, originally published 1539)

Vives, J.L, *The Education of a Christian Woman: a sixteenth century manual*, (edited and translated by Fantazzi, C, (University of Chicago Press, 2000, initially written 1523)

Journals

Asso, C, 'Erasmus, Desiderius', *Encyclopedia of Renaissance Philosophy*, M. Sgarbi (ed.), (Springer Nature Switzerland AG, 2020)

Baldwin, J, 'The Evolution of the Public School', *Educational Weekly*, Vol. 1, No.4, pp.3-4, (Sage Publications Inc, 1883)

Carlson, D.R., 'Royal Tutors in the Reign of Henry VII', *The Sixteenth Century Journal*, Vol.22, No.2, Summer (1991)

Cravathy, P.D, 'Gray's Inn', *American Bar Association Journal*, Vol. 10, No. 1, (January 1924), p. 19-21

Ellis, R, 'The Juvenile Translations of Elizabeth Tudor', *Translation and Literature*, Vol. 18, No. 2, (Autumn 2009) p. 157-180

Flood, John, L, 'Poets Laureate of the holy Roman Empire', *Hungarian Journal of English and American Studies* (HJEAS), Vol. 3, No. 2, BRITISH STUDIES ISSUE (1997), p. 5-23

Friedman, A.T, 'The Influence of Humanism on the Education of Girls and Boys in Tudor England', *History of Education Quarterly*, Vol. 25, No.1/2, (Spring-Summer, 1985), p. 57-70

Howard, P, 'Juan Luis Vives: Early Innovator in Education', *Bethlehem University Journal*, Vol.6, (1987)

Rand, E, *The School Review*, Vol. 18, No.7, (The University of Chicago Press, 1910)

Roche, J.R & Thomas, P, 'A Library for a Sixteenth-Century Gentleman', *The Princeton University Library Chronicle*, Vol. 38, No. 2/3, (The Robert H. Taylor Collection, Winter-Spring, 1977), p.120-133

Sills, K.C.M, 'Virgil in the Age of Elizabeth', *The Classical Journal*, Vol. 6, No. 3, (December 1910), p. 123-131

Watson, F, 'Vives on Education', *The Journal of English and Germanic Philology*, April 1915, Vol. 14, No. 2, (University of Illinois Press, 1915)

Secondary Sources

Ackroyd, P, *The History of England: Vol II, Tudors*, (MacMillan, London, 2012)

Alford, S, *Edward VI*, (Penguin, London, 2014)

Baldwin Smith, L, *Elizabeth Tudor, Portrait of a Queen*, (Hutchinson & Co, London, 1976)

Barber, N, *Tudor England*, (Raintree, 2005)

Barber, N, *History in Art: Tudor England*, (White-Thompson Publishing, 2005)

Barratt, J, *Ludlow's Last Prince, Prince Arthur 1486-1502*, (Ludlow Friends Trust)

Bingham, J, *The Tudors: The Kings and Queens of England's Golden Age*, (Arcturus Publishing Ltd, London, 2018)

Borman, T, *Elizabeth's Women*, (Vintage, London, 2010)

Borman, T, *The Private Lives of the Tudors*, (Hodder & Stoughton, London, 2017)

Breverton, T, *Everything You Ever wanted to Know About the Tudors But Were Afraid to Ask*, (Amberley, Stroud, 2014)

Brimacombe, P, *Life in Tudor England*, (Pitkin Guide, Jarrold Publishing, 2004)

Bruce, M.L., *The Making of Henry VIII*, (William Collins Sons & Co Ltd, London, 1977)

Bryson, A, *Cheke, Sir John (1514–1557), humanist, royal tutor, and administrator*, (Oxford Dictionary of National Biography. Retrieved 2 Jan. 2022, from https://www.oxforddnb.com/view/10.1093/ref:odnb/9780198614128.001.0001/odnb-9780198614128-e-5211.)

Bryson, S, *La Reine Blanche*, (Amberley, Stroud, 2018)

Chancellor, V.E., *Medieval and Tudor Britain*, (Penguin, London, 1969)

Childs, E, *William Caxton, A Portrait in a Background*, (Northwood Publications Ltd, London, 1976)

Chrimes, S. B., *Lancastrians, Yorkists and Henry VII*, (MacMillan & Co Ltd, London, 1966)

Clegg, M, *Margaret Tudor*, (Pen and Sword, Barnsley, 2018)

Coward, B, *Social Change and Continuity in early Modern England 1550-1750*, (Longman Group, Harlow, 1995)

Cressy, D, *Education in Tudor and Stuart England*, (Edward Arnold, London, 1975)

Cunningham, S, *Prince Arthur, The Tudor King Who Never Was*, (Amberley, Stroud, 2016)

De Lisle, L, *Tudor: The Family Story*, (Vintage Books, London, 2014)

Dickens, A. G & Jones, W. R. D, *Erasmus the Reformer*, (Methuen, London, 1994)

Doran, S, *The Tudor Chronicles: 1485-1603*, (Quercus Publishing Plc, London, 2011)

Dover Wilson, J, *The Schools of England: A Study in Renaissance*, (Sidgwick & Jackon Ltd, London, 1928)

Draskau, J. K., *The Tudor Rose*, (The History Press, Stroud, 2013)

Duffy, E, *The Stripping of the Altars, Traditional religion in England 1400-1580*, (Yale University Press, London, 1992)

Dunn, J, *Elizabeth and Mary*, (Harper Perennial, London, 2003)

Elton, G. R., *England Under The Tudors: History of England, Vol. IV*, (Methuen & Co Ltd, 1962)

Froude, J. A., *Life and Letters of Erasmus, Lectures Delivered at Oxford 1893-4*, (Longmans, Green and Co., London, 1902)

Gairdner, J, *Henry the Seventh*, (MacMillan & Co Ltd, London, 1909)

Gassner, J, *Medieval and Tudor Drama*, (New York, 1971)

Goodman, R, *How to be a Tudor*, (Penguin, London, 2015)

Gordon, P & Lawton, T, *Royal Education, Past, Present and Future*, (Frank Cass, London, 1999)

Gristwood, S, *Game of Queens*, (Oneworld, London, 2017)

Guy, J, *A Daughter's Love*, (Harper Perennial, London, 2009)

Guy, J, *The Children of Henry VIII*, (Oxford University Press, Oxford, 2013)

Guy, J, *Henry VIII,* (Penguin, London, 2014)

Hart-Davis, A, *What the Tudors and Stuarts did for us*, (Boxtree, London, 2002)

Hexter, J. H, *Reappraisals in History*, (Longmans, Green & Co Ltd, London, 1961)

Hibbert, C, *The English Social History 1066-1945*, (Harper Collins, London, 1994)

Hilton, L, *Elizabeth, Renaissance Prince*, (Weidenfield & Nicolson, London, 2014)

Hutchinson, R, *Young Henry*, (Phoenix, London, 2012)

Innes, A, *A History in England: England Under the Tudors*, (Methuen, London, 1920)

Ives, E, *Henry VIII,* (Oxford University Press, London, 2007)

Jewell, H. M, *Education in Early Modern England*, (MacMillan Press Ltd, London, 1998)

Jones, N, *The Birth of the Elizabethan Age, England in the 1560s*, (Blackwell Publishers, Oxford, 1993)

Kewley Draskau, J, *The Tudor Rose*, (The History Press, Stroud, 2013)

Kintgen, E, *Reading in Tudor England*, (University of Pittsburgh Press, Pittsburgh, 1996)

Kipling, G, *Duwes [Dewes], Giles [pseud. Aegidius de Vadis] (d. 1535), musician and royal tutor*, (Oxford Dictionary of National Biography. Retrieved 28 Nov. 2021, from https://www.oxforddnb.com/view/10.1093/ref@odnb/9780198614128.001.0001/odnb-9780198613128-e-7575.)

Knight, C, *William Caxton, a Biography*, (London, 1976)

Knighton, T & Fallows, D, *Companion to Medieval & Renaissance Music*, (Oxford University Press, Oxford, 1992)

Lacey, R, *The Life and Times of Henry VIII*, (Weidenfield & Nicholson, London, 1992)

Lawson, J & Silver, H, *A Social History of Education in England*, (Methuen, London, 1973)

Lawson, J, *Castiglione, Giovanni Battista [alias John Baptist Castillion] (c. 1515-1598), Italian tutor*, (Oxford Dictionary of National Biography. Retrieved 28 Nov. 2021, from https://www.oxforddnb.com/view/10.1093/ref@odnb/9780198614128.001.0001/odnb/9780198614128-e-76297.)

Lewis, C. S, *The Discarded Image*, (Cambridge University Press, 1964)

Lloyd, D, *Arthur Prince of Wales*, (Ludlow, 2002)

Loades, D, *Henry VIII, Court, Church and Conflict*, (The National Archives, Surrey, 2009)

Loades, D, *Mary Tudor*, (Amberley, Stroud, 2012)

Loades, D, *Henry VIII*, (Amberley, Stroud, 2013)

Lockyer, R, *Tudor and Stuart Britain: 1471-1714*, (Longman, Harlow, 1985)

MacCulloch, D, *The reign of Henry VIII: Politics, Policy and Piety*, (Palgrave, Hampshire, 1995)

Mackie, J. D., *The Earlier Tudors: 1485-1558*, (Oxford University Press, London, 1966)

Marshall, R. K., *Elizabeth I*, (HMSO, London, 1991)

Martienssen, A, *Queen Katherine Parr*, (Sphere Books Ltd, London, 1975)

Matusiak, J, *Henry VIII, The Life and Rule of England's Nero*, (The History Press, Stroud, 2014)

Matz, R, *Defending Literature in Early Modern England, Renaissance Literary Theory in Social Context*, (Cambridge University Press, Cambridge, 2000)

McGrath, A, *Christian Theology*, 4th ed., (Blackwell Publishing, Oxford, 2007)

McRae, A, *Renaissance Drama*, (Arnold, London, 2003)

Miller, H, *Henry VIII and the English Nobility*, (Basil Blackwell Ltd, Oxford, 1989)

Mortimer, I, *The Time Traveller's Guide to Elizabethan England*, (Vintage Books, London, 2013)

Mumby, F. A., *The Youth of Henry VIII*, (Houghton Mifflin, New York, 1913)

Murphy, B, *Bastard Prince, Henry VIII's Lost Son*, (Sutton Publishing Ltd, Stroud, 2001)

Nelson, W, *A Fifteenth Century School Book from a Manuscript in the British Library (Ms. Arundel249)*, (Oxford, 1956)

Norton, E, *The Tudor Treasury*, (André Deutsch Ltd, London, 2014)

Norton, E, *The Temptation of Elizabeth Tudor*, (Head of Zeus, London, 2015)

Norton, E, *The Lives of Tudor Women*, (Head of Zeus, London, 2017)

O'Day, R, *Ascham, Roger (1514/15-1568), author and royal tutor*, (Oxford Dictionary of National Biography. Retrieved 28 Nov 2021, from https://www.oxforddnb.com/view/10.1093/ref:odnb/9780198614128.001.0001/odnb-9780198614128-e-732.)

Orme, N, *English Schools in the Middle Ages*, (Methuen, London, 1973)

Orme, N, *Education and Society in Medieval and Renaissance England*, (The Hambledon Press, London, 1989)

Orme, N, *Medieval Children*, (Yale University Press, London, 2003)

Orme, N, *From Childhood to Chivalry, The Education of the English Kings and Aristocracy 1066-1530*, (Routledge, Oxon, 2018)

Orme, N, *Holt, John (d. 1504), schoolmaster and grammarian*, (Oxford Dictionary of National Biography. Retrieved 2 Jan. 2022, from https://www.oxforddnb.com/view/10.1093/ref:odnb/9780198614128.001.0001/odnb-9780198614128-e-13617.)

Penn, T, *Winter King*, (Penguin, London, 2012)

Perkins, K, *The Education of Princess Mary Tudor*, (LSU Master's Theses, 2007)

Perry, M, *Sisters to the King*, (André Deutsch Ltd, London, 2002)

Pincombe, M, *Elizabethan Humanism: Literature and Learning in the later Sixteenth Century*, (Longman, London, 2001)

Plowden, A, *The House of Tudor*, (The History Press, Stroud, 2010)

Pollard, A. F, *Henry VIII*, (Jonathan Cape, London, 1970)

Pollard, A. J., *Late Medieval England: 1399-1509*, (Pearson Education Ltd, London, 2000)

Pollard, A. W & Redgrave, G.R, *A Short-Title Catalogue of Books Printed in England, Scotland, & Ireland And of English Books Printed Abroad 1475-1640*, (The Bibliographical Society, London, 1948)

Pollintz, A, *Princely Education in early Modern Britain*, (Cambridge University Press, 2015)

Porter, L, *Mary Tudor*, (Piatkus, London, 2007)

Porter, S, *Everyday Life in Tudor London*, (Amberley, Stroud, 2016)

Quennell, M & C. H. B, *A History of Everyday Things in England 1066-1799*, (Charles Scribner's Sons, New York, 1918)

Reeves, C, *Pleasures & Pastimes in Medieval England*, (Alan Sutton Publishing Limited, Stroud, 1997)

Rex, R, *Henry VIII*, (Amberley, Stroud, 2009)

Ridley, J, *The Tudor Age, (Constable & Co. Ltd, London, 1998)*

Rowse, A. L., *A Man of Singular Virtue being A Life of Sir Thomas More by his son-in-law William Roper and a selection of More's letters*, (The Folio Society, London, 1980)

Scarisbrick, J. T, *Henry VIII*, (Yale University Press, London, 1997)

Seebohm, F, *The Oxford Reformers*, (J.M. Dent & Sons Ltd, London, 1914)

Sharpe, J. A, *Early Modern England, A Social History 1550-1760*, (Hodder Headline, London, 1997)

Shuter, J, *The Poor in Tudor England*, (Heinemann, Oxford, 1995)

Sim, A, *Pleasure and Pastimes in Tudor England*, (Sutton Publishing, Stroud, 1999)

Sim, A, *The Tudor Housewife*, (The History Press, Stroud, 2010)

Simon, J, *Education and Society in Tudor England*, (Cambridge University Press, Cambridge, 1967)

Skidmore, C, *Edward VI, The Lost King of England*, (Phoenix, London, 2008)

Somerset, A, *Elizabeth I*, (Orion Books, London, 1997)

Starkey, D, *Elizabeth*, (Chatto and Windus, London, 2000)

Starkey, D, *Henry*, (Harper Perennial, London, 2009)

Starkey, D & Greening, K, *Music and Monarchy*, (Random House, London, 2013)

Stein, G, *Palsgrave, John (d. 1554), teacher and scholar of languages*, (Oxford Dictionary of National Biography. Retrieved 2 Jan. 2022, from https://www.oxforddnb.com/view/10.1093/ref:odnb/9780198614128.001.0001/odnb-9780198614128-e-21227.)

Stevens, J, *Music & Poetry in the Early Tudor Court*, (Methuen, London, 1961)

Thompson, C, *Schools in Tudor England*, (Folger Shakespeare Library, The University of Virginia, Virginia, 1973)

Warnicke, R, *Women of the English Renaissance and Reformation*, (Greenwood Press, London, 1983)

Watkins, S, *Margaret Tudor Queen of Scots*, (Chronos Books, Hants, 2017)

Watson, F, *The Old Grammar Schools*, (Cambridge University Press, London, 1916)

Weir, A, *The Children of Henry VIII, (Ballantine Books, 1996)*

Whitelock, A, *Mary Tudor: England's First Queen*, (Bloomsbury, London, 2010)

Williams, N, *The Life and Times of Henry VII*, (George Weidenfield & Nicholson Ltd, London, 1994)

Williams, P, *The Later Tudors: England 1547-1603*, (Oxford University Press, London, 1995)

Wilson, D, *Shire Living Histories: Tudor England*, (Shire Publications Ltd, 2010)

Wooding, L, *Henry VIII*, (Routledge, Oxon, 2015)

Woodward, W. H, *Studies in Education During the age of the Renaissance*, (Cambridge University Press, Cambridge, 1906)

Notes

Abbreviations

CSPV – Calendar of State Papers, Venetian
CSPS – Calendar of State Papers, Spain
ELR – Edward VI, Literary Remains
LPFD – Letters & Papers Foreign and Domestic in the reign of Henry VIII.

Introduction

1. Orme, N, *English Schools in the Middle Ages*, Methuen & Co Ltd, London, (1973), p. 59-60.
2. Porter, S, *Everyday Life in Tudor London*, Amberley, Stroud, (2016), p. 62.
3. Pollard, A.J., *Late Medieval England 1399-1509*, London, (2000), p. 388.
4. Goodman, R, *How to be a Tudor*, London, (2015), p. 108.

Chapter One – Educating Henry

1. Borman, T, *The Private Lives of the Tudors*, London, (2017), p. 43.
2. Hutchinson, R, *Young Henry*, Phoenix, London, (2012), p. 16. Fourteen shillings were paid for horses for Henry on 1 January 1494.
3. Ibid, p.36. Henry VII paid £1 on 2 November 1494 for the book.

4. Skelton, J, *The Complete English Poems*, ed. J. Scattergood, Penguin, London, (1983), p. 132.
5. Cicero, Marcus Tullius, *Commentum familiare in Ciceronis officia*. Lyon, 1502. The copy is held at the Folger Shakespeare Library, Washington, USA. (See images)
6. Skelton, J, *Speculum Principis,* reproduced in Salter, F.M. (ed), Speculum, Vol, IX. No.1 (January 1934), pp. 25-37.
7. Hutchinson, R, *Young Henry*, Phoenix, London, (2012), p.36. Skelton gave the book to Henry in 1511 and it is now preserved at Cambridge University and can be viewed digitally with its inscription and annotations by Skelton under the reference Corpus Christi College MS 432.
8. Ibid, p. 39. *Prosopopeia Britanniae* was published in 1500, dedicated to Henry.
9. Borman, T, *The Private Lives of the Tudors*, London, (2017), p. 69.
10. 'Spain: August 1504', in *CSPS, Volume 1, 1485-1509*, ed. G A Bergenroth, London, (1862), p. 398
11. Orme, N, *English Schools in the Middle Ages*, Methuen & Co Ltd, London, (1973), p. 110.
12. Guy, J, *Henry VIII*, Penguin, London, (2014), p. 10.
13. Starkey, D, *Henry*, Harper Perennial, London, (2009), p. 180.
14. Hutchinson, R, *Young Henry*, Phoenix, London, (2012), p. 93.
15. Rowse, A.L., *A Man of Singular Virtue being A Life of Sir Thomas More by his son-in-law William Roper and a selection of More's Letters*, The Folio Society, London, (1980), pp. 33-34.
16. Lacey, R, *The Life and Times of Henry VIII*, Weidenfield & Nicolson, London, (1992), p. 20.
17. Carlson, David. R, 'Royal Tutors in the reign of Henry VII', *The Sixteenth Century Journal*, Summer 1991, Vol. 22, No. 2 (Summer, 1991), p. 274.
18. Report of Sebastian Giustinian, the Venetian ambassador on his first visit to England, 'Henry VIII: July 1519, 16-29', in *Letters and Papers, Foreign and Domestic, Henry VIII, Volume 3, 1519-1523*. Ed. J.S. Brewer, London (18670, p. 136-148, f.2.

19. Henry VIII's Songbook is in the British Library and contains thirty-three pieces believed to have been composed by Henry VIII.

Chapter Two – Royal Children

1. André, B, *The Life of Henry VII*, Translated by Hobbins, D, (Translation of *Historia regis Henrici Septimi, by Bernard Andreas; edited by James Gairdner; published by Longman, Brown, Green, Longmans and Robert, 1858),* Italica Press, New York, (2011), p. 10.
2. Starkey, D, *Henry*, Harper Perennial, London, (2009), p. 119.
3. Cunningham, S, *Prince Arthur, The Tudor King Who Never Was*, Amberley, Stroud, (2016), p. 27.
4. André, B, *The Life of Henry VIII*, Translated by Hobbins, D, (Translation of *Historia regis Henrici Septimi, by Bernard Andreas; edited by James Gairdner; published by Longman, Brown, Green, Longmans and Robert, 1858),* Italica Press, New York, (2011) pp. 38-39.
5. Ibid, p. 39
6. Cunningham, S, *Prince Arthur, The Tudor King Who Never Was*, Amberley, Stroud, (2016), pp. 61-62. It is likely Arthur, like Henry, learnt to ride at a very young age.
7. *Privy Purse Expenses of Elizabeth of York*, ed. N.H. Nicolas, London, (1830), p. 28.
8. Perry, M, *Sisters to the King*, André Deutsch Ltd, London (2002), p. 43.
9. The Education Act 1496 was an act of Parliament in Scotland. Eldest sons of barons and landowners were required to attend school to study law, the arts and Latin.
10. Watkins, SB, *Margaret Tudor Queen of Scots*, Chronos Books, Hants, (2017), p. 4, originally referenced in Strickland, A, *Lives of the Tudor Princesses*, London, (1868).

11. During the Tudor Age the new year did not start until 25 March. This was changed to the current Gregorian Calendar by Pope Gregory XIII in 1584 but this would mean Mary was born in 1496 using today's calendar,

12. Bryson, S, *La Reine Blanche*, Amberley, Stroud, (2018), p. 34. Juana was the elder sister of Katharine of Aragon and inherited the throne of Castile upon Isabella's death.

13. LPFD, Henry VIII, 1509-47, Vol.1, Part iii, pp. xxxvii-xxxviii.

14. Perry, M, *Sisters to the King*, André Deutsch Ltd, London (2002), p. 57. Margaret Beaufort had a French attendant in her household, Perrot Doryn who Mary also could have practiced with.

Chapter Three – All the King's Children

1. Sir Francis Bryan was certainly not a vicar and received the nickname from Thomas Cromwell, it was also used by Henry VIII. Bryan was a patron of Greek scholars although he was unable to translate manuscripts himself, he was intrigued by the subject and humanist learning.

2. Guy, J, *The Children of Henry VIII*, Oxford University Press, Oxford, (2013), p. 25.

3. Ibid, p. 40.

4. Wooding, L, *Henry VIII*, Routledge, Oxon, (2015), pp. 21-22.

5. Guy, J, *The Children of Henry VIII*, Oxford University Press, Oxford, (2013), p. 44.

6. Ibid, p. 60.

7. Murphy, B.A. *Bastard Prince: Henry VIII's Lost Son*, Sutton Publishing Limited, Stroud, (2001), pp. 70-1.

8. LPFD, IV, ii, no. 2081.

9. Ibid, IV, iii, no. 5806(ii) Palsgrave to Henry VIII.

10. Ibid, IV, ii, no. 3135; Fitzroy Inventory, p. xxxvii-xli

11. Ibid, IV, ii, nos. 3860-1.

12. *Letters of Roger Ascham*, ppp. 210-11.

13. Ascham, R, *English Works*, ed. W.A. Wright, Cambridge University Press, London, (1904), p. 216-217.
14. Ibid, pp. 245-246.
15. Wooding, L, *Henry VIII*, Routledge, Oxon, (2015), p. 22.
16. *The Chronicle and Political Papers of King Edward VI*, ed. W.K. Jordan, George Allen and Unwin Ltd, London (1966), p. 3.
17. Cheke is said to have owned eight of Hans Holbein's sketches and portraits, these would be the perfect material for a prince to learn who is who in the nobility so he may recognise them at court.
18. Alford, S, *Edward VI*, Penguin Monarchs, London, (2014), p. 17. Edward quoted *'magistrum metue'* meaning 'fear (or respect) your teacher in a letter to his tutor Richard Cox.
19. Borman, T, *The Private Lives of the Tudors*, London, (2017), p. 210.
20. Alford, S, *Edward VI*, Penguin Monarchs, London, (2014), p. 29.
21. Letter from Roger Ascham to Johannes Sturm, December 1550, *ELR,* p. cli-clii.
22. Ackroyd, P, *The History of England, Volume II: Tudors*, Macmillian, London, (2012), pp. 147-148.
23. CSPV, 1534-1554, pp. 535-6.
24. Ellis, R, *The Juvenile translations of Elizabeth Tudor*, Translation and Literature, Vol. 18. No. 2, Edinburgh University Press, (2009), p. 157.

Chapter Four – Tutors of the Tudors

1. Orme, N, *English Schools in the Middle Ages*, Methuen & Co Ltd, London, (1973), pp. 107-109.
2. Porter, S, *Everyday Life in Tudor London*, Amberley, Stroud, (2016), p. 61.
3. Ridley, J, *The Tudor Age*, Constable & Co Ltd, London, (2002), pp. 188-189.
4. André, B, *The Life of Henry VIII*, Translated by Hobbins, D, (Translation of *Historia regis Henrici Septimi, by Bernard*

Andreas; edited by James Gairdner; published by Longman, Brown, Green, Longmans and Robert, 1858), Italica Press, New York, (2011) p. 39.

5. Carlson, D. R, 'Royal Tutors in the Reign of Henry VII', *The Sixteenth Century Journal,* Vol. 22, No. 2, (Summer, 1991), p. 259. André refers to Rede as *'optimus et doctissimus praeceptor'.* The translation is kindly provided by D.R. Carlson in the referenced journal article.

6. Edwards, A.S.G, *Skelton: The Critical Heritage,* London, (1981), p. 44.

7. Doran, S, *The Tudor Chronicles,* Quercus, London, (2011), p. 82.

8. Starkey, D, *Henry,* Harper Perennial, London, (2009), p. 121 and Flood, J, 'Poets Laureate of the Holy Roman Empire', *Hungarian Journal of English and American Studies* (HJEAS), Vol. 3, No. 2, British Studies Issue, (1997), pp. 5-23.

9. An excerpt from *Garland or Chapelet of Laurel,* the full poem along with other works of Skelton can be found at https://www.exclassics.com/skelton/skel061.htm

10. Starkey, D, *Henry,* Harper Perennial, London, (2009), pp. 174-5.

11. Carlson, D. R, 'Royal Tutors in the Reign of Henry VII', *The Sixteenth Century Journal,* Vol. 22, No. 2, (Summer, 1991), p. 271.

12. Ibid, p. 272.

13. The series formed part of Paulo Giovio's *Descriptio Britanniae a "Vivorum aliquot in Britannia qui nostro seculo erudition et doctrina clari memorabilesque fuerunt elogia"* published in 1548.

14. Edwards, A.S.G, *Skelton: The Critical Heritage,* London, (1981), p. 62.

15. Kipling, G. Duwes [Dewes], Giles [pseud. Aegidius de Vadis] (d. 1535), musician and royal tutor. *Oxford Dictionary of National Biography.* Retrieved 2 Jan. 2022, from https://www.oxforddnb.com/view/10.1093/ref:odnb/9780198614128.001.0001/odnb-9780198614128-e-7575.

16. Howard, P, *Juan Luis Vives: Early Innovator in Education,* Bethlehem University Journal, Vol. 6, (August 1987), p. 59.

17. Ibid, pp. 64-65.
18. Alford, S, *Edward VI*, Penguin Monarchs, London, (2014), p. 15.
19. Ascham, R, *English Works*, ed. W.A. Wright, Cambridge University Press, London, (1904), p. 183.
20. Williams, N, *The Life and Times of Henry VII*, Weidenfield & Nicolson, London (1994), p. 130.
21. Foxe would have been required to take holy order following a year of delivering public lectures. As a Protestant, this was against his beliefs.
22. The Field of Cloth of Gold took place in France and was a meeting between Henry VIII and Francois I, King of France which lasted around three weeks and was in effect a huge pageant and display of wealth on both sides.

Chapter Five – Educating the Aristocracy

1. Orme, N, *Education and Society in Medieval and Renaissance England*, The Hambledon Press, London, (1989), pp. 163-164.
2. Quennell, M & C.H.B., *A History of Everyday Things in England 1066-1799*, Charles Scribner's Sons, New York (1918), p. 24.
3. Orme, N, *English Schools in the Middle Ages*, Methuen & Co Ltd, London, (1973), p. 70.
4. Rummel, E, (ed.), *The Erasmus Reader*, University of Toronto Press, Toronto, (1990), pp. 86-97.
5. Law French was a dialect of Norman French and English phrases that was still sometimes used in treatises or recording of proceedings. A skill likely required for reading historical judgements.
6. *Records of the Honourable Society of Lincoln's Inn: Black Books Volume 1, 1422-1585,* p. 105.
7. Ibid, pp. 108-109.
8. Guy, J, *A Daughter's Love*, Harper Perennial, London, (2009), pp. 59-65, 67-70, 140-3.

9. Ibid, pp. 156-7.

10. Guy, J, *The Children of Henry VIII*, Oxford University Press, Oxford, (2013), p.4 3.

11. Hibbert, C, *The English, A Social History 1066-1945*, Harper Collins, London, (1994), p. 273.

Chapter Six – Educating the Common People

1. Lawson, J & Silver, H, *A Social History of education in England*, Methuen, London, (1973), pp. 69-70.

2. Horman's vulgar was printed privately for the pupils of Eton School.

3. Nelson, W, ed. *A Fifteenth Century School Book, From a Manuscript in the British Museum (Ms. Arundel 249)*, Oxford University Press, London, (1956), pp. 2-21.

4. Williams, N, *The Life and Times of Henry VII*, Weidenfield & Nicolson, London, (1994), p. 138.

5. Simon, J, *Education and Society in Tudor England*, Cambridge University Press, Cambridge, (1967), p. 75.

6. Colet, J. Dean, *Statutes of Dean Colet: Founder of St. Paul's School... also, A copy of the will of Sir T. Gresham...dated...1575...added, the names of a few eminent persons who were educated at St. Paul's School...* J. Hatchard and J. Richardson, London, (1816), p. 12.

7. Froude, J. A, *Life and Letters of Erasmus, Lectures Delivered at Oxford 1893-4*, Longmans, green and Co, London, (1902), p. 105.

8. Lawson, J & Silver, H, *A Social History of Education in England*, Methuen, London, (1973), pp. 61-62.

9. Orme, N, *English Schools in the Middle Ages*, Methuen & Co Ltd, London, (1973), p. 48.

10. Sim, A, *The Tudor Housewife*, The History Press, London (2010), p. 100.

11. Lawson, J & Silver, H, *A Social History of Education in England*, Methuen, London, (1973), p. 123.

Chapter Seven – Religion as Education

1. Wooding, L, *Henry VIII*, Routledge, Oxon, (2015), p. 46. Originally printed in Boorde, A, *A Compendyous Regyment or a Dyetary of helth* (1557), ed. F.J. Furnivall (EETS 32, 1868), p. 246.
2. Guy, J, *The Children of Henry VIII*, Oxford University Press, Oxford, (2013), p. 39.
3. The cycle of plays came to an end in 1580.
4. Reeves, C, *Pleasures & Pastimes in Medieval England*, Alan Sutton Publishing Ltd, Stroud, (1997), p. 82.
5. Orme, N, *English schools in the Middle Ages*, Methuen & Co Ltd, London, (1973), p. 12.
6. Wooding, L, *Henry VIII*, Routledge, Oxon, (2015), pp. 81-82.
7. Hibbert, C, *The English, A Social History 1066-1945*, Harper Collins, London, (1994), p. 279.
8. Starkey, D, *Henry*, Harper Perennial, London, (2009), p. 201.
9. Sim, A, *Pleasure &Pastime in Tudor England*, Sutton Publishing Limited. Stroud, (1999), p. 128.

Chapter Eight – Books, Music & Drama

1. A copy of *Prayers and Meditations* can be seen at Sudeley Castle which was also the home of Katheryn Parr and where her tomb can also be seen.
2. *The Book of the Ordre of Chyvalry* was translated from French to English by Caxton. The original was written by the Catalan philosopher Ramón Lull in the thirteenth century.
3. Sim, A, *Pleasure & Pastimes in Tudor England*, Sutton Publishing Limited, Stroud, (1999), p. 132.
4. Ridley, J, *The Tudor Age*, Constable & Co Ltd, London, (2002), pp. 164-166.
5. Sim, A, *Pleasure & Pastimes in Tudor England*, Sutton Publishing Limited, Stroud, (1999), p. 120.

6. Erasmus, D, *The Education of a Christian Prince*, ed. L, Jardine, Cambridge, (1997), p. xxi-xxii.
7. *The Boke of St Albans* is attributed to Dame Juliana Barnes whilst the author of *The Treatyse of Fysshynge with an Angle* is unknown.
8. Quennell, M & C. H. B., *A History of Everyday Things in England 1066-1799*, Charles Scribner's Sons, New York, (1918), p. 69.
9. Bruce, M. L., *The Making of Henry VIII*, Collins, London, (1977), p. 26.
10. The British Library holds a manuscript called *Henry VIII's Songbook* which contains 109 pieces of music. Thirty-four of these are attributed to Henry. The manuscript is referred to as B.L. Additional MS 31922.
11. Hutchinson, R, *Young Henry*, Phoenix, London, (2012), p. 200.
12. Sim, A, *Pleasure & Pastimes in Tudor England*, Sutton Publishing Limited, Stroud, (1999), pp. 110-11.
13. Doran, S, *The Tudor Chronicles*, Quercus, London, (2011), pp. 316-318.
14. Castiglione, B, *The Book of the Courtier*, originally published in Venice, 1528. Translated by Leonard Eckstein Opdycke, New York (2203), pp. 84-5.
15. Ridley, J, *The Tudor Age*, Constable & Co Ltd, London, (2002), p. 261.
16. Borman, T, *The Private Lives of the Tudors*, London, (2017), p. 140.

Chapter Nine – Pastimes for All

1. Wilson, D, *Shire Living histories: Tudor England*, Shire Publications Ltd, (2010), p. 67. The Act was determined to maintain class division, prevent possible unrest and rioting and maintain the practice of archery.
2. Ascham, R, *English Works*, ed. W.A. Wright, Cambridge University Press, London, (1904), p. 217.

3. Letter to Cardinal Wolsey from *'Letters and Papers, Foreign and Domestic of the Reign of Henry VIII'*, Quoted from Thurley, *The Royal Palaces*, p. 191.

4. This was declared in an act of Parliament in 1485 by Henry VII. If poachers disguised their faces, it was also punishable by death. Daylight or undisguised poachers were fined or imprisoned for trespassing.

5. Sir Thomas Elyot, *The Book Named the Governor*, (1531), pp. 66-7.

6. Bruce, M.L., *The Making of Henry VIII*, Collins, London, (1977), p. 36.

7. Goodman, R, *How to be a Tudor*, London, (2015), p. 197.

8. Borman, T, *The Private Lives of the Tudors*, London (2017), p. 137.

9. Reeves, C, *Pleasure & Pastimes in Medieval England*, Allan Sutton Publishing Limited, Stroud, (1997), p. 95.

10. Ackroyd, P, *The History of England, Volume II: Tudors*, Macmillian, London, (2012), p. 147.

11. Goodman, R, *How to be a Tudor*, Penguin, London, (2015), p. 195.

12. Sim, A, *Pleasures & Pastimes in Tudor England*, Stroud (1999), p. 78. Advent was a period of fasting for the Tudors beginning on Advent Sunday four weeks prior and ending Christmas Day.

13. Ibid, p. 90.

14. Ibid, p. 88.